Disciples of Jesus

Learning to Serve Like Jesus

Dr Bob Gordon

Sovereign World

Sovereign World
PO Box 777
Tonbridge
Kent, TN11 0ZS
England

ISBN: 1 85240 199 0

Typeset by CRB Associates, Reepham, Norfolk
Printed in England by Clays Ltd, St Ives plc.

Preface

The preparation of these study manuals has been an exciting team adventure. It has been my privilege over the past few years to produce a number of books dealing with the subjects of discipleship, ministry and leadership. This has found a particular focus in two major volumes; *The Foundations of Christian Living* and *Master Builders*, both published by Sovereign World International. This material has become a major focus of our whole ministry and today those two volumes are published in a number of different languages.

Recently it has become even more clear that there is a growing need for material which will help Christians grow in life and develop in ministry. All over the world there is a phenomenal growth in numbers of new believers. Amongst more established believers there is a new hunger to progress in maturity both in life, and in an understanding of their faith.

These volumes are offered as part of the answer to this growing need. They began life as a pilot scheme devised by the leader of our team in the Netherlands, Kees de Vlieger. The effect throughout many churches and in the lives of many believers has been profound. Now they have been revised, remodelled and expanded in the confidence that they will reach a much wider market and meet a much greater area of need.

I am so grateful to the team who have helped get them this far, in particular, to Kees de Vlieger for his inspiration. Andrew Whitman helped with the completion of certain study notes and his wife Rosie and Anne Holmes did a good job with final proof reading. Simon Smailus, who prepared the manuals for their final production, deserves a special mention for the many dedicated hours he has put in compiling and correcting the text ready for final printing.

The last word must go, of course, to God our Father without whose help and blessing none of this would ever happen.

Bob Gordon

CONTENTS

Introduction

This is the third of three manuals which have been produced together to provide a progressive and interesting study guide to growth in Christian life and ministry. The first focuses on certain basic essentials for personal Christian life and growth. The second considers some important lessons if we are to be effective in our ministry for Jesus. The third examines vital insights with regard to our call as servants of the Kingdom of God.

The goal of this particular study is to increase our awareness of the call of God and to learn some important lessons about working this out in our lives.

Self-esteem, power, authority and leadership are words which are held in high regard among many pundits in our world today. Jesus has much to say about these very issues. But the basis on which he lived and taught was quite different from what we learn from the world around us. His words from Matthew 20:26–28 were important in the preparation of the material in this manual:

> 'Whoever wants to become great among you must be your servant, and whoever wants to be first must be your slave – just as the Son of Man did not come to be served, but to serve, and to give his life as a ransom for many.'

The first two chapters look at the principles and nature of our call. These are followed by an important exercise of spiritual self-examination before God which will help us to become more aware of areas where adjustment is needed. The next few chapters deal with spiritually practical areas about our use of time and the positive benefits of practising the presence of God. The heart of this study in the following four chapters helps us to recognise important principles of growth, how to face problems and pressure, and how to overcome the challenges we face with God's help. The final two chapters help everyone who does this course to appreciate their own place in the service of God which, of course, is a vital principle of fruitfulness.

Our prayer is that everyone who does this study will be stimulated and helped to know and develop their call in God in a more effective way.

Bob Gordon

Kees de Vlieger

and Team

How to make the most of this manual

There are two ways in which this manual can be used:

1. ***Individually***
    This is working through the sections at your own pace at home. There are twelve sections and it is suggested that you complete one section a week.

2. ***As a group***
    If you intend to use this manual for group study then we recommend that you purchase a copy of the *Group Leaders Manual* which has been specifically designed for this purpose. The *Group Leaders Manual* gives clear instructions on how to make the most of this material. It shows what material to teach each week and what homework to set. This is done by a detailed twelve-week plan contained in the *Group Leaders Manual*.

Some recommendations

- Before you start the manual ask yourself the question; 'Do I really want to be a true disciple of Jesus?' If you do, then it is important to take this course seriously and to commit yourself to finishing it. Look ahead and see yourself as God desires you to be, and how you can be more fruitful in your service for Him. Determine to grow in your maturity in Christ.

- Do not approach the study in a hurried way. Take your time in looking up the Scripture and answering the questions, especially if you are studying this course alone. Commit each teaching unit to the Lord in prayer and ask God to speak to you through it. Meditate upon relevant sections and try to apply the truths learned to your daily life. This is how to grow in maturity as a disciple of Jesus.

- If you are studying this course as part of a group, determine to be an integral part of that group. The word *fellowship* comes from the Greek word **koinonia** which means *to share things in common.* Your growth as a disciple of Jesus will be greatly helped by the encouragement that others can be to you. Learn to trust them and then share your life with them. Share with others in the group the things you are learning about God and His Word. In this way you will be able to live together in much of what you study and so your faith will increase and you will grow in your maturity in Christ.

- As one of a group you will get most out of the course by reading and studying the teaching unit well before the group actually meets together. This will give you time to meditate on the various truths and begin to apply them to your life. Questions arising can then be discussed and the truths more readily understood as the leader of the group progresses through the teaching unit as he feels led of God.

SECTION 1
The Call of God

Introduction

God's General Call to All Christians

All Christians, in a general sense, are called by God (2 Thessalonians 2:13, 14). We are called by God out of the kingdom of darkness into God's Kingdom (1 Peter 2:9). We are saved from eternal separation from God and given eternal life with Him (1 John 5:11, 12). We have been called to live as disciples of Jesus (Matthew 28:18–20) and, as such, we have been called by God to obey Him and to carry out the work that we alone have been created by Him to achieve (Jeremiah 1:4–10; Ephesians 2:10).

There is no such thing as unemployment in the Kingdom of God. God has a work for every one of His people. This does not mean, however, that we will always have a clear job description from God. At times, we may not know specifically what He wants us to do for Him; perhaps because He wants us to learn to trust Him or wait on Him or even to take a rest.

Christians who have been given no clear directive from God, need to get on and do the things they see need to be done. Too many Christians look for a label before they do anything for God. God asks us to get on and prove faithful in the little things and, if we do our best to obey Him, He will progressively reveal His will for our lives, i.e. our label.

In today's world, we like to pigeon-hole everything, but God never promises to do this. At times, we may not even be able to put a label on our call, but we should deep down know that we are doing what God wants us to do.

> *'Set your minds, then, on endorsing by your conduct the fact that God has called and chosen you.'*
> (2 Peter 1:10 J.B. Phillips)

Key Verses

1 Peter 2:9   Proverbs 3:5, 6

John 15:5–8   Romans 12:3

Ephesians 2:10   2 Timothy 1:6

PART 1.1
Discernment of Call

One major weakness in some current approaches to teaching about discernment of spiritual giftings and callings, is the amount of responsibility which is laid at the door of the person concerned.

God does not always call the most likely or even the most humanly gifted people. There is a mystery about God's call that can only be answered in the heart of God. In fact, God often calls the unlikely into positions of authority (1 Corinthians 1:26, 27). This humbling, sobering thought reveals that we need to be totally dependent on God, never relying on our natural talents alone.

It will be helpful if we always bear the following *four important principles* in mind when we speak of being called of God.

i)   A sense of call

Many people in the church today mix up the wish to do something for God with God's actual call to do it. Some Christians even try to force the issue by going to Bible college or by pushing themselves into a spiritual position in their local church for example. This is never any substitute for God's call. Of course, the Scriptures tell us to desire the best gifts, but that desire should never override the reality of the call of God to a specific and unique ministry.

The sense of God's call on our lives may start as a little thing, but it grows. A real call of God is like a seed planted in a field; it does not die but grows if given half a chance. Until we get a sense of God's call and until we know that now is the time for that call to be outworked, we should get on with life, doing what God has already shown us to do.

ii) A heart for the work

God usually gives us a desire for the work after He has called us to do it. We need to be able to discern the difference between longing or desire to serve the Lord and knowing the call of God. A call is productive because it leads to action, but desire does not.

This may not be evident at first, but as we move into our call in God, there will be nowhere else we would want to go and nothing else we would rather do. It will be burning in our bones (Jeremiah 20:9).

A heart for the work does not mean that we will enjoy every experience we will have in our ministry for God. Often the burden for the work will lie so heavily upon us that it will seem as though it will break us. Sometimes we will experience frustration when we realise how much there is to be done, and how little we can give to meet the demand. Nevertheless, to the person whom God calls, these things act as a stimulus to the spirit and lead to greater dedication to the task.

iii) Exercise of gift

A person's ministry makes room for itself. A real call of God will manifest itself in the exercise of it. God does not appoint and anoint into inertia. There is an in-built dynamic in the call of God through which it will continually find expression in practice.

A call from God evidences a sort of spiritual ambition within the heart. This is not an ambition of the flesh or self-interest, but a desire that comes from God. A desire to be going on in the work, and to find the means and outlets for what is inside us to be fulfilled in practice. This spiritual drive (not strive!) is integral to a real call of God and is what leads a person forward to take the steps that are necessary to bring the work to fruition.

iv) Fruitfulness

So many people lay claim to ministry in advance of fruitfulness, when, in fact, fruitfulness is the real sign of ministry. God's grace is always effective and it produces fruit in us and in the lives of those to whom we minister. Effectiveness is the real witness to the fact that we are called and gifted by God.

> *'Do not neglect your gift, which was given you through a prophetic message when the body of elders laid their hands on you.'*   (1 Timothy 4:14)

> *'Fan into flame the gift of God.'*   (2 Timothy 1:6)

> *'Each one should use whatever gift he has received.'*
> (1 Peter 4:10)

PART 1.2
God's Timing

i) The right time

Many Christians run ahead of God and step out into their call before it is His time to do so. We need to wait on the Lord and move into our calling only when the Lord so directs. The anointing from God we will need to fulfil our call will then be evident. Trying to step into a call outside of God's timing necessitates striving, because we will have to work at a job in our own strength.

Some people may try and push you forward before your time. Do not yield to this! It is important to follow God's leading alone, because very often His timing is contrary to man's wisdom.

It is also important not to resist God when the timing is right. Remember the words of Mordecai to Esther in Esther 4:14:

> *'Who knows but that you have come to royal position for such a time as this?'*

Mordecai believed that another would be raised up if Esther did not respond as she should to God's call on her life at that time. God does not always do things as we would plan them; we need to stay open to God. Let us not miss out on what God has planned for us.

As we progress in our Christian walk, one lesson we should learn quickly is that God's timing is perfect. Take care never to rush ahead of God (Psalm 32:8, 9; Proverbs 3:5, 6).

ii) Some of us are not quite ready

The Bible abounds with people who were really called by God, but who underwent a period of preparation and waiting before God brought them into their place of call, e.g. Jesus was 30 before He entered His ministry, David was a shepherd and then a leader in exile before ascending to the throne of Israel, and Moses was 40 years in Pharaoh's courts and 40 years in the wilderness before he was ready to lead the children of Israel. We need to learn to wait on God (Psalm 27:14).

iii) The real thing

Nobody can make up a call from God. A call to ministry is like a seed: it has the shape, essence and colour of the ministry within it. When we are called by God to a ministry, He places within us all we need to operate fruitfully and successfully within that call. Our responsibility is just to nurture that call and let it grow at God's pace by simply being obedient to God in whatever He asks us to do. God will open the doors for us to be able to fulfil our call at the right time and when we are ready.

PART 1.3
Confirming a Call

There should be evidence in our experience that God has actually witnessed to our call by His Holy Spirit. When there is a particular call, there is usually confirmation from outside ourselves. Reason, feelings and emotions can lie to us at times, so we cannot rely on these.

Some ways to confirm a call from God include:

- If you suspect a call, do not just go to a friend who always agrees with you and who will automatically underwrite it, but wait on God and go to people you can be sure will seek the Lord with you on the matter.

- God's provision can confirm a call, because God does not call and then not equip.

- God can speak to us through the Scriptures to confirm a call.

- A call is also supported by the fact that you may be working effectively and fruitfully in a certain way for the Lord. Here, people are confirming your call by responding to it and being helped. After all, the Kingdom of God is not a matter of talk, but of power (1 Corinthians 4:20). It is no good saying you have a call, if the door does not open and people do not respond to it. A call to leadership should generate ministry activity of the sort to which we are called and also be effective and fruitful in this area.

- You should know the call of God on your life before anyone else. You will not need other people to tell you what to do. Others should only confirm what you already know from God. It should be within you and the only question is: Are you going to risk walking in it? God's will born in you is the greatest thing that you possess.

- If we have given our lives over to God, He will lead and guide us. We will not need a formula to discover His will or the call He has placed on our lives. God's will and call, to people who whole-heartedly follow Him, is like a fire burning in their bellies which will not go away, no matter what anybody says to them.

PART 1.4
Content with Our Call

God has a special and unique plan for every one of His servants. The knowledge of this should stop any believer from envying the ministry of other people who, after all, only differ in function because of God's divine plan. Every Christian needs to be content with the calling God has placed on their life.

Being true to this call will be the best thing that person can do with their life. God knows what we are like; He knows what will fulfil us; He knows what needs to change in us; and He knows what He needs to take us through. We need to trust Him with our lives and obey whatever He asks us to do for Him.

When we know what our call is and we rest in that, we will not be threatened by the call that God places on anybody else's life. We will be content with what God has for us and we will be able to help other people in their call. True unity comes within the church as we recognise and affirm the different calls that God places on our lives, and not as we all become the same.

PART 1.5
Enabling the Call

i) Our choices and commitments

The choices and commitments we make in life have a great deal to say about the extent to which God's call will be effective in us. Many individuals ruin or inhibit the call which God has given them by showing a lack of concern, care or wisdom in the decisions they make in vital areas of their lives.

The choices we make in every fundamental area of our life, such as our use of time, the partner we choose, what we do with the opportunities presented to us, and so on, all have an important bearing on whether or not we will ever come near to realising God's potential for our lives. Even the organisational structures in which we choose to work should never be there just for the sake of it, but rather be servants of the call of God on our lives.

ii) Remaining teachable

In order to be fruitful in our call, we must remain teachable and be open to the power of God. Just because we have been called to do something for God, does not mean we have arrived. We are only just beginning!

Our capacity to fulfil our call is only partly developed when we are first called by God. We need to grow in capacity as we outwork our call. It does not matter who is called by God, and what their background is, if they live within their call as God desires, they can achieve great things and quite remarkable capacities for God.

iii) Be true to your calling

One of the main reasons that people do not live in the good of the calling that God places on their lives is that they live in unreality. We need to be specific about what we take on, because we need to be true to our calling. To do otherwise will crush us, because we will be taking on pressures that we will have no resources in God to resist (1 John 2:20, 27).

This requires us to think in sober, realistic terms about ourselves in God (Romans 12:3).

iv) A call can be lived in

A call from God usually has written within it an inner recognition that we will be equipped for this call. Those who are called may feel inadequate or unworthy, but they need to know that in God they have what it takes to respond fully to their call. They will even be able to cope with any training or discipline that may be necessary.

Many people may feel that they are not the right ones for the job. They do not see how God can use them, so they run away from their call. God, however, sees the potential work we can do for Him when we are clothed with the Holy Spirit. He knows us better than we know ourselves; we just need to trust Him.

v) A call must be lived in

A call must be lived in and not just left on the shelf. This is because God is looking for faithful people who will walk in obedience to Him, and because we need to operate in a calling in order to sharpen it and make it more effective.

Too many Christians are lazy within their calling and want God to do everything, instead of disciplining their lives and regarding the calling as a talent that must be stewarded well (Matthew 25:14–30). Others let their call get swamped in the midst of their busy life and, therefore, give it no time to operate.

The good news is that God's call is irrevocable (Romans 11:29). If we have not lived in our call as we should, we need to ask God to forgive us, and then we need to pick up the pieces and begin again.

vi) Spreading yourself too thinly

One big mistake often made by the church as a whole is the training of people to do a general function, like being a vicar or pastor, where they have to cover a multitude of callings. Here, they spread themselves so thinly that they never fully achieve anything. People who act like this also prevent others around them from fulfilling their call because they seem to leave no room for other people to fulfil their calling in God.

vii) We may not know the full picture

God does not usually reveal His total plan for our ministry all at once, because He knows that if we saw some of the things we were going to go through, we may give up before we start.

All of God's servants can be assured that God will show them everything they need to know when they need to know it. He has also promised to give them everything they need to meet every situation they are likely to face, if they look to Him in those situations.

Bible Study: *The Call of God*

God's general call

1. As Christians, we are called accordingly to:

    _____ _____ (Romans 8:28)

2. Read Romans 8:29. In your own words, what is His purpose?

    _____

    _____

    _____

3. Look at the following verses/passages. What does God's calling result in?

    a) 1 Peter 2:9 _____

    b) Hebrews 3:1 _____

    c) 1 Thessalonians 2:12 _____

    d) Philippians 3:12–14 _____

    e) Colossians 3:15 _____

    f) 2 Peter 1:10 _____

    g) 2 Thessalonians 2:13–14 _____

    _____

    According to 2 Thessalonians 2:13–14, what does it mean to 'share in the glory of our Lord Jesus Christ'?

    _____

    _____

    _____

4. God gives us the resources we need to fulfil His calling. Look up these two verses: Philippians 4:13 and 2 Peter 1:3.

What does 'everything' refer to in each verse?

_____

_____

_____

God's specific call

Individuals called

5. In the Old Testament: *Jeremiah*
(Jeremiah 1:4–10)

What different aspects do you notice about the prophet's calling?

a) _____

b) _____

c) _____

d) _____

e) _____

Which apply to you?

_____

Which do not apply to you?

_____

_____

_____

6. In the New Testament: *Timothy*
    (1 Timothy 4:14 & 2 Timothy 1:6)

    a) How did Timothy's call come?

    _____

    _____

    b) What was his calling?

    _____

    _____

    c) Why was Timothy flagging in his calling?

    _____

    _____

Christians called

7. According to the following verses what are we called to?

    a) Ephesians 2:10 _____

    _____

    b) 2 Timothy 1:9 _____

    _____

Pause for Thought

Pause to reflect and jot down the following:

*   Which 'good works', is God currently calling you to?

*   Which gifts is God currently calling you to exercise?

---

8. How we use our gift is also important. We should use them with a sense of:

    _____ (Romans 12:3)

    _____ (Matthew 25:14–30)

Looking further at the above verses:

9.   In what ways are our use of gifts affected by:

   a)   Our view of ourselves (Romans 12:3)?

   _____

   _____

   _____

   b)   Our view of God's character (Matthew 25:24–25)?

   _____

   _____

   _____

10. In a sentence write down what you think God's calling is for you at the moment:

   _____

   _____

Answers

1. His purpose

2. His purpose is for us to become more like the Lord Jesus
    Christ

3. God's calling results in our:
    a) speaking out God's praise
    b) giving Jesus our attention
    c) living life in a godly manner
    d) pressing on to perfection
    e) letting God's peace rule in our hearts
    f) adding character traits (verses 5–7) to our faith
    g) sharing in the glory of our Lord Jesus Christ

    Here Paul seems to be referring to the future glory of Jesus
    – when he comes again to be 'glorified in his holy people'
    (1:10). This will involve, for example, relief from trouble
    and judgement for those who troubled us (1:6–7), together
    with the overcoming of 'the lawless one' (2:8).

4. • *Philippians 4:13*: Material resources – whether well
       provided for or in particular need.

    • *2 Peter 1:3*: Spiritual resources – godly living as part
       of our relationship with God.

5. a) he was prepared for it before his birth
    b) he was appointed to address the nations
    c) he responded to it with great reticence
    d) he was reassured by the presence of God
    e) he was given the Lord's words to speak

    Apply: All except (b), to one degree or another.

    Do not apply: In specific terms (b), because this was a
    particular feature of Jeremiah's calling. However, together
    with all Christians, we are called to take the gospel to all
    nations (e.g. Matthew 28:18–20).

6. a) Through a prophetic message and the laying on of hands.
    b) To lead the church in Ephesus by (i) example and (ii) teaching (1 Timothy 4:12, 13).
    c) Probably because he thought he was too young age-wise (1 Timothy 4:12) and too timid ministry-wise (2 Timothy 1:7).

7. a) Express God's work in us by doing good works.
    b) Demonstrate God's salvation by living a holy life.

8. Realism

    Responsibility

9. a) If we think too much of ourselves we may end up attempting to do more than God has enabled us to.
    b) If we think He is a 'hard task-master' this could lead to fear in using our talents, and even to not using them at all.

10. Personal

SECTION 2
Called as Servants

Introduction

No rights of our own

A servant is a person who is not his own master; he serves another master. Put another way, a servant is a person who lives without the right to fulfil his personal will; he exists to do the will of his master. In fact, a true servant has no rights of his own that he can demand.

Servants of God are those who have dethroned themselves and everything else in their life and experience, and enthroned Jesus and made Him Lord of all their life. This means they put Jesus first in everything and they do not serve riches, power, possessions, or anything else that is contrary to God's will (Matthew 6:24). Instead of putting God first in everything, most Christians withhold something. They may say with their lips that 'Jesus is Lord', but they do as they please in many areas of life. When Jesus is truly Lord of our lives, we will never say 'no' to Him when He asks us to do something for Him, no matter how costly.

> *'So then, men ought to regard us as servants of Christ and as those entrusted with the secret things of God. Now it is required that those who have been given a trust must prove faithful.'* (1 Corinthians 4:1, 2)

Even those called to leadership in the Body of Christ are not lords because everybody in that Kingdom has only one Lord, Jesus Christ (1 Corinthians 8:6). In God's Kingdom, those who lead other people are the servants of those people. In fact, Christian leaders should set the example of being a servant of God, by serving Him and the people for whom they are responsible, wholeheartedly. God's leaders should be able to say to those who follow them, 'Imitate me', because they are imitating Christ and walking as He did (1 Corinthians 11:1; 1 John 2:6).

Jesus said,

> *'Let him who is the greatest among you become as the youngest, and him who is the chief and leader as one who serves.'* (Luke 22:26 Amplified Bible)

Key Verses

Exodus 21:2–6

Philippians 2:5–8

Matthew 6:24

Colossians 3:15–16

Romans 6:6–18

1 Peter 2:21–23

PART 2.1
Who Do We Serve?

The truth is that everybody serves a master, either the devil or God (Matthew 6:24; John 8:34–36; John 15:19; Romans 6:6–22; James 4:4; 1 John 2:15–17; 1 John 4:4–6); there is no middle ground. We are either under the dominion of sin and the devil, or we have been ransomed by Jesus Christ and we are now His servants (Galatians 1:10). There is no possible way that we can pay back the Lord Jesus Christ for what He has done for us, therefore our only recourse is to serve God with all our heart.

In today's western society we rarely, if ever, think of ourselves as serving anybody. The majority of people put themselves first in most, if not everything, they do. They are, therefore, in grave danger of serving (or even becoming slaves of) their own selfish desires.

Whatever takes up most of our time and energy is that to which we have given our heart. This is what we really serve. If these things are in line with God's will they are alright, but if not, we are allowing other things or people to be lord, at least in an area of our lives. We need to put God first in everything and make accomplishing His will the number one priority of our lives (1 Peter 2:21; Philippians 2:5–8).

When we see ourselves as nothing but God's servants, there is very little that can get in the way of our doing God's will and of our being channels of the Holy Spirit. When we become something in our own eyes, we stop being just servants of God's will and we start doing what we think is right. The things we decide to do may be good ideas, but the power of the Holy Spirit will not flow and enable these things, because they are not the will of God. The Holy Spirit only moves in power when the will of God is being carried out (Galatians 2:20).

> *'Now fear the Lord and serve him with all faithfulness. Throw away the gods your forefathers worshipped beyond the River and in Egypt, and serve the Lord. But if serving the Lord seems undesirable to you, then choose for yourselves this day whom you will serve, whether the gods your forefathers served beyond the River, or the gods of the Amorites, in whose land you are living. But as for me and my household, we will serve the Lord.'*
> (Joshua 24:14, 15)

PART 2.2
Jesus Our Example of Servanthood

S lavery was basic to the ruling Roman society at the time of Jesus. Slaves were well treated generally, but they were non-persons. The Greeks and the Jewish authorities saw slavery as demeaning and shameful. The Greeks felt it was their life's aim to fully achieve their potential. Being forced to subject their will or surrender their time and effort for another was unthinkable. The Jewish authorities thought of themselves as those chosen by God to rule. They were, therefore, not there to serve other people, but to be served as they served God. It was into this context that Jesus spoke His words about servanthood.

Jesus said,

> *'For even the Son of Man did not come to be served, but to serve, and to give his life as a ransom for many.'*
> (Mark 10:45)

We can learn what servanthood and humility really are from Jesus and by following His example (John 13:1–17; Philippians 2:5–11). For Jesus, being nothing in Himself was a way of life.

Servanthood became a way of life for Him long before He saw the cross. He really was someone, but He made Himself nothing. Jesus called Himself the servant of all and yet He was and is, the name above all names, who knew the ways of God's power in an immediate and personal sense. He brought life out of death more than once during His earthly ministry; when He touched men they were made well; when He spoke, demons trembled and fled.

> *'Your attitude should be the same as that of Christ Jesus: Who, being in very nature God, did not consider equality with God something to be grasped, but made himself nothing, taking the very nature of a servant, being made in human likeness. And being found in appearance as a man, he humbled himself and became obedient to death – even death on a cross!'*
>
> (Philippians 2:5–8)

PART 2.3
True Servanthood is Powerful

i)   The best example

Jesus was the ultimate example of humility and servant-hood and yet He was the most powerful man who ever lived. The truth is though, that Jesus had the same power available to Him as we have to us – the Holy Spirit.

Jesus understood that the Holy Spirit only moved in power when God the Father released Him to do so. Therefore, Jesus submitted His life totally to the will of God the Father and He did nothing but the will of God. This is true servanthood (John 5:19). This gave Jesus His authority and power, because He knew that when He did as His Father wanted, the Holy Spirit would act in power on His behalf. Jesus became, therefore, a channel for the releasing of God's will. Whenever He saw the Father doing something, He knew that He could do it on earth in the power of the Holy Spirit. When Jesus spoke, it was as if the Father spoke and when He acted, it was as if the Father was acting.

ii) We can live the same way

We are called to follow the example of Jesus (1 Corinthians 11:1; 1 Peter 2:21; 1 John 2:6). If we, as born-again, Spirit-filled Christians, discover the will of God and become its servant, God will release the power of His Holy Spirit to enable His will to be done. Nothing will be impossible, because nothing is impossible to God (Luke 1:37; 18:27). To do this, we need to live lives that are totally submitted to the will of God; then we too will be channels through which God can bring about His will. God will show us what to do if we make ourselves available to Him.

iii) The secret of power

We can see the secret of God's power in the experience of Jesus. We receive the Spirit of God only by measure: the Father is just as willing to give us the Spirit, but the limitations of our own hearts determine the measure of the Holy Spirit in us. We are so full of garbage and self-concern that there is not room for the Spirit in great measure. Hurts, pride, selfishness and rebellion inhibit our hearts and prevent the Holy Spirit from having room to work within us. The truth is that there were no denizens of darkness within the heart of Jesus. There was room for God to pour in the Spirit without measure (John 3:34).

Most Christians do not give God enough room in their lives and they are not servants of the will of God. These two factors are the main reasons for the power failure in the church today. We can not serve God in the way that He asks us to in our own strength. We need to discover God's will and then step out in faith, knowing that God's power will enable His will to be done.

We should never do things just because they seem good at the time. We should regard ourselves as nothing but God's servants, having no rights and making no demands. If we do this, there will be nothing to stand in the way of the power of God being released in order to achieve God's will.

iv) **No striving**

There is no striving when you are living as a true servant of God. You can rest in God if you know that He will take care of all the details of your life as you do His will (Matthew 6:25–34; Hebrews 4:1–11; 2 Peter 1:3). Life becomes simple: God speaks, we obey, it happens. Of course, there is a cost to such a life as can be evidenced in the life of Jesus, but for the Christian, there is no other way to live, if we want to be really effective for God. Our flesh (i.e. body and soul) also battles against such a way of life, because it is unable, in itself, to live a life of faith. We need to discipline our lives and allow God to renew our minds in order to attain this quality of walk with God.

Jesus said,

> *'Take my yoke upon you and learn from me, for I am gentle and humble in heart, and you will find rest for your souls. For my yoke is easy and my burden is light.'* (Matthew 11:29, 30)

PART 2.4
Signs That We Are Acting as a Servant of God

A Hebrew slave was to be released after six years, unless at that time, he chose to remain with his master's family. If he did wish to remain, his ear was pierced with an awl in the sight of the judges of a city as a sign that he was a servant for life (Exodus 21:2–6; Deuteronomy 15:12–18). As Christians, our lives should be a sign to others that we are servants of Jesus Christ. Some of the signs that we are acting as servants include:

- We will be seeking first the Kingdom of God (Matthew 6:33).

- We will be a servant of all (Matthew 20:26–28).

- We will look to our Master to reward us (Matthew 25:21).

- We will be serving others and, in doing so, be serving the Lord Jesus Christ (Matthew 25:31–40).

- We will deny ourselves, take up our cross daily and follow our Master, Jesus (Luke 9:23).

- We will be following the example of Jesus and so living an unselfish life, serving rather than being waited upon (Luke 22:27).

- We will give generously, because we know it is more blessed to give than to receive (Acts 20:35).

- We will be faithful when entrusted with something (1 Corinthians 4:2).

- We will carry the burdens of others (Galatians 6:2).

- We will be humble, gentle, patient, and we will bear with other people in love (Ephesians 4:2; 1 John 3:11–24).

- We will work at everything wholeheartedly, because we always work for the Lord and not for men (Colossians 3:23, 24; Ephesians 6:6–8).

- We will look to the interests of others, as well as our own interests (Philippians 2:4).

- We will want to please our Lord in all we do (2 Timothy 2:4).

PART 2.5
Meeting the Needs of Others

Good servants know the needs of those they serve and how to meet those needs. They even try to anticipate the needs of those they serve, so that they can be ready and prepared to meet those needs. Christian leaders must learn what the appropriate response is to a situation and they must learn when to minister this response. This may mean reaching out and touching those to whom this is appropriate; hugging another; weeping or laughing with another; or ministering to another by the laying on of hands etc.

PART 2.6
A Willing Spirit

i) Willingness to do the menial

God's servants must never be too proud to get stuck in and do the little jobs that need to be done. Some of us are called to serve the Word and others are called to serve the tables (Acts 6:1–7). When each part of the body of Christ does its bit, serving God in the way He asks them to, no matter how menial the task, then we today will see what the early church saw; an increase in power and in numbers. No task should ever be regarded as too menial for God's leaders to lower themselves to, if they are true servants of God.

ii) Serving those over us

Every Christian is called to serve Jesus Christ, who is the head of His Body, the Church (Ephesians 5:23). Those called to leadership in particular need to set the example in this area. They must also be committed to serve those who are over them in leadership.

iii) Serving with the right motivation

The most effective Christian workers are those who want to serve God because they know Him and love Him. Such people do not serve for money, position, reputation, power, fame or any other selfish motivation. These sorts of people are also able to put in far more effort, take on board far more pressure, and sacrifice far more, than those who work in God's church for any other reason. They are not out to prove themselves, and therefore they are secure, resting in their relationship with God.

iv) Serving with joy

We are called to serve with joy, because God does not want service grudgingly given. He wants us to serve Him whole-heartedly. If we can serve God with joy, it helps to keep us sane, to keep our motivation right, to maintain the peace of

God ruling in our hearts as it should (Philippians 4:4–7; Colossians 3:15–17); and it helps us to keep the right attitude of heart as we serve.

True servants of God realise that the source of their joy is serving God and other people, rather than serving themselves and their own selfish desires. To be mostly concerned with attaining your own joy or happiness is contrary to having a servant heart.

> *'Never be lacking in zeal, but keep your spiritual fervour, serving the Lord.'*   (Romans 12:11)

PART 2.7
The Gifts of Service

The gifts of the Spirit are gifts of service to the Body of Christ (1 Corinthians 12:4–11). These gifts are not given to exalt anybody or to give us power for our own sake; they are given that we, as God's servants, might be enabled or empowered to serve the Body of Christ, in whatever way is necessary. We all have a responsibility to administer these gifts faithfully, so that the Body of Christ is built up and the Kingdom of God is extended.

> *'Each one should use whatever gift he has received to serve others, faithfully administering God's grace in its various forms. If anyone speaks, he should do it as one speaking the very words of God. If anyone serves, he should do it with the strength God provides, so that in all things God may be praised through Jesus Christ. To him be the glory and the power for ever and ever. Amen.'*
>
> (1 Peter 4:10, 11)

PART 2.8
Servants Are Raised Up by God

If we take the last place and serve God and others first, and if we have no rights that we demand, God has promised to lift us up to the best possible place for ourselves (Matthew 20:25–28; Matthew 23:11, 12; Mark 9:35; Mark 10:43, 44).

So we need to humble ourselves before God (1 Peter 5:6). Humility is not grovelling about in the dust. It is living as Jesus did, being a servant, submitting yourself to the will of God and doing only it (Luke 14:11 and John 6:38). Jesus was no weak worm, He was the most powerful man who ever lived.

We need to see ourselves as God sees us, both as servants and sons at the same time. We, in ourselves, are nothing, and but for the grace of God, we would still be nothing. We owe everything we are and have to Him. We need to entrust our lives to our faithful God.

Jesus said,

> 'I tell you the truth, unless an ear of wheat falls to the ground and dies, it remains only a single seed. But if it dies, it produces many seeds. The man who loves his life will lose it, while the man who hates his life in this world will keep it for eternal life. Whoever serves me must follow me; and where I am, my servant also will be. My Father will honour the one who serves me.'
>
> (John 12:24–26)

Personal Notes

Assignment

Who/what do you serve?

1. Answer the following questions as honestly as you can. In this way you can begin to ascertain who or what you really serve.

   a) Who/what comes *first* in your life?

   _____

   _____

   b) Which activities occupy most of your time?

   _____

   _____

   _____

   c) What would be the *last* thing you would give up?

   _____

   _____

   d) What is your heart really set on (having, achieving, etc.)?

   _____

   _____

   _____

   e) How do you determine the budgeting of your money?

   _____

   _____

   _____

   f) What is uppermost in your mind most of the time?

   _____

   _____

g) Are there any 'masters' you serve other than Jesus? (see Matthew 6:24)

_____

_____

_____

2. Using your answers above, try and fill in the box below giving an honest idea of what your priorities are *at the moment*.

My actual priorities right now are as follows:

1) _____

2) _____

3) _____

4) _____

5) _____

---

3. *Now take a good break before coming back to the second box.*

Here the idea is to jot down what our biblical priorities as Christians should be. From the most important downward. You may like to put a scripture verse or passage alongside each of these priorities.

My biblical priorities as a Christian should be:

Scripture

1) _____   _____

2) _____   _____

3) _____   _____

4) _____   _____

5) _____   _____

---

4.   Comparing the two boxes on the previous page, what adjustments do I need to make in my lifestyle?

_____

_____

_____

How willing are you to serve?

5.   Every now and again assess yourself by asking the following questions. To make this practical, rate each answer on a scale of 1–10 (1 = definitely not!; 10 = definitely so!). Put your score in the box provided. In this way you can monitor your progress over time.

a)   Am I willing to be God's servant and for this to be the controlling factor of my life?

b)   Am I willing every day, to pay the price of being a servant to others?

c)   Am I willing to live a disciplined lifestyle, and to be an example to others in this?

d)   Am I secure enough in God to serve others gladly and yet still be positive about myself (seeing myself as Christ sees me)?

e)   Am I willing to give all that I am and have to God, and to do all that He asks of me?

f)   Am I willing to allow those I serve to reach their full potential in Christ, even if they outstrip me in some area?

g)   Am I willing to learn from others and not be the person with all the answers, thus strengthening my friendship with those I lead?

Summary

Reflecting on all the above exercises, complete the following sentence in your own words.

I would like to be the type of a servant who:

_____

_____

_____

Personal Notes

Answers

1. Personal

2. Personal

3. My biblical priorities as a Christian should be:

		Scripture
1)	God	Matthew 22:37
2)	Family	1 Timothy 5:8 (cf Mark 7:9–13)
3)	Church	Galatians 6:10
4)	Work	Colossians 3:22–4:1
5)	Leisure	Exodus 20:8–11

You will probably need to give this further thought and consideration. For example, do you actually agree with the priority list above? Perhaps you think that 3 and 4 ought to be swapped around, or that there are some occasions where 3 should take precedence over 2.

4. Personal

5. Personal

SECTION 3
A Spiritual Check-up

Introduction

Honest to God

F rom time to time, it is a good exercise to take an honest look at ourselves. Many people find it difficult and even fear to be objective about who or what they are. Such fears need to be laid aside, because an important factor in our personal development is the spiritual honesty that tells us who we are and how we tick. Failure in the area of self-assessment and self-awareness contributes a great deal to lack of achievement in important areas of life. Leaders, in particular, need to be self-aware people.

As Christians, we need to be real with ourselves. God cannot be fooled. He knows who we are, so there is no point pretending to be something or someone else in our dealings with Him. This is the starting point for getting our act together with God. If we fool ourselves into thinking we are something when we are not, we will be dangerous both to ourselves and to others.

This section is designed to assist Christians to be more aware of themselves. *We all need to increase our awareness of*:

- our strengths and weaknesses

- how we will react in the various situations that we come across

- how to make room for God within our experience

- how to stay available for God's use, no matter what situation confronts us

Key Verses

1 Samuel 16:7

Romans 8:16, 17

Galatians 5:22–25

Philippians 3:12–14

2 Timothy 1:7

2 Peter 1:3–8

PART 3.1
We Need to Grow in Christ

'Man looks on the outward appearance, but the Lord looks at the heart.' (1 Samuel 16:7)

I f a baby doesn't develop after a year or two in certain recognised areas, we say there is something malfunctioning or there is something deficient about that baby's development. We begin to be concerned that the baby will not grow into a mature human being as an adult. We do not only look at the physical development of the child to make such an assessment, we look at the child's mind and its capacity to function; and we look for signs of the development of its perception, personality and character. Sadly, we have all seen people being wheeled around in wheel-chairs who, although they have fully grown physically, have failed to develop in strategic areas of their personality. This, unfortunately, is like many Christians. They look all right on the outside, but in *three big areas of development they have not grown*. *These three areas are*:

- *Moral development* – This is when a person's character grows because they are beginning to perceive the difference between right and wrong, i.e. they are beginning to make moral choices.

- *Intellectual development* – This is the ability of an individual to understand knowledge, and then retain it, communicate it and make use of it.

- *Gift/capacity development* – This is the capacity of an individual to discern who they are and what they can do. It is also the putting to use of these capacities.

These are areas that we all need to grow in as Christians. Too many Christians have gifts that are vitiated or disabled because of major character flaws. Other Christians, who have developed their moral character tremendously, do not seem to be able to perceive God's will for their lives and so they are never fruitful for God. As Christians, we need to be well-rounded in our personality, especially in these three areas of development.

A spiritual check-up

The following five sections highlight five important areas in which any Christian needs to grow if he or she is ever going to be really effective for God.

PART 3.2
Self-awareness

'May God himself, the God of peace, sanctify you through and through. May your whole spirit, soul and body be kept blameless at the coming of our Lord Jesus Christ. The one who calls you is faithful and he will do it.'   (1 Thessalonians 5:23, 24)

Many of the problems associated with our growth as Christians stem from the fact that *we have not come to terms with ourselves*. We do not know who we are, and therefore over the years we create or build up a whole shell of unreality around our lives. This has the effect of masking who we really are, causing us to live in unreality.

Christians *must not be frightened of self-assessment*. They must not cover up honesty with spiritual language. As Christians, we need to be real when it comes to questions about our effectiveness. What have our efforts produced? What money is really available? How many people did come to the Lord last year and how many of them are still going on with the Lord? We often cover up such questions by saying we must not be critical or negative, when in fact, all these questions attempt to do is get us to be honest.

Christians *suffer from many hurts, pains and aggravations at physical, emotional and spiritual levels* as a result of a wrong self-assessment. They have a bad self-image and they only seem to notice reactions from other people that reinforce this. For example, it is amazing how often Christians think a person dislikes them, when in fact, the person is very positive towards them.

Insecurity is the cause of most of our incorrect opinions of ourselves. We need to learn how to be comfortable with ourselves. It isn't about how slim, big, short, or tall we are; or whether we are extrovert or introvert; what really counts is who we are to God and what we are expressing to others.

A lot of Christians *only do things at a surface level*. They put on a show for those around them so that they will be seen to be spiritual people. God wants us to be real with Him and each other. He does not want *poseurs* who do all the right things. He wants real people who are right with Him in heart. He wants people who are honest with Him and with themselves. He wants us all to think of ourselves as He does; not too highly (Romans 12:3) or with a bad self-image (Romans 8:16, 17).

As Christians, *we need to learn how to cope with our imperfect selves*. When we were filled with the Spirit of God, we did not lose all our imperfections. God wants us to improve in these areas, but He also knows that we are who we are and that it will take time to improve. We need to press on to perfection (Philippians 3:12) with God's help, but we must not live in condemnation in the meantime. The Scriptures say that there is absolutely no condemnation for those who are in Christ (Romans 8:1, 2).

Too many Christians *only see the magnitude of the problem* when they do any form of self-assessment and it obliterates them. Other Christians refuse to believe they have a problem and they attempt to cover up any weaknesses they may have, instead of coming to terms with them. These are not God's ways. He wants to look at the problems with us and to come up with achievable answers. He even promises to give us all we need to achieve His will in our lives (2 Peter 1:3; Philippians 4:19).

God wants us to know how we 'tick', so that we can modify our behaviour and live a life that glorifies Him. For example, if we have a temper, He doesn't want us to ignore this. He would rather we learned what triggered the temper and avoided such triggers with His help. We need to learn what happens inside us when we are confronted with a particular circumstance or stimulus, because then we can learn how to respond to it in a godly way. In order to do this, we need to understand ourselves and we need to make room for God to help us in the situation. He wants our reactions to be right and He will do all He can to help us to change.

Over time, *we will find that the godly reactions become our normal ones*. Situations or stimuli that once would have caused us great trouble, will no longer be a problem to us. While this process is going on, God does not want us to lock ourselves away from the world; He simply wants us to get on with the work He has set before us.

We need to *see ourselves as God sees us*, because this is who we really are. We may be able to mask things from ourselves, but nothing can be hidden from Him. Even if what we see is not good, God will not leave it this way. He wants to take us all on to a place of security in Him. He wants us to grow in our relationship with Him and to mature as Christians.

> The starting point for such growth is discovering who we are and then yielding what needs to be changed over to God.

If we never see the problems and weaknesses, because we are covering them up all the time, we will never grow in God. We also need to get over the hill of our own self-negativism which destroys our confidence before God, because without confidence in God we will never be able to minister in power.

One thing we must not do, however, is constantly look at ourselves. We must never become neurotic or obsessed with ourselves. Too many people make self-assessment their life-time hobby. This is a self-centred approach to self-assessment and it is not what God wants us to do as Christians. He wants us to come to Him, so that He can to show us the truth about ourselves and our work. Too many Christians fail in this area and are ineffective for God, because they cannot see beyond themselves and their problems. God wants us to live in personal freedom so that we will be fruitful for Him and so that we can live the abundant life He promised (John 10:10).

Pause for Thought

We **can begin to develop a sense of self-awareness** by asking the sort of simple questions that follow. Take a moment or two to think about them before moving on.

- How do I function?

- What is my personality like?

- What sort of self-image do I have?

- What are my pluses and minuses?

- What are my fears?

- What is my attitude towards people I like/ dislike or activities I enjoy/find difficult etc.?

PART 3.3
Self-discipline

'For God did not give us a spirit of timidity, but a spirit of power, of love and of self-discipline.'   (2 Timothy 1:7)

Self-discipline is not the same as the English disease of the 'stiff upper lip'. Self-discipline is achieved in the power of the Holy Spirit. We can do all things through God who gives us strength (Philippians 4:13). In fact, self-control is one part of the fruit of the Spirit (Galatians 5:22, 23).

Not many Christians achieve anything like their full potential in God. Most of us never get anywhere near as far intellectually, spiritually, physically, personally, relationally, socially, or motivationally as we should. There are too many of us who would prefer to take a back-seat and let others do the work. We do not want the discipline of life that is called for in order to achieve what God wants us to achieve for Him.

If you look at a car battery from the top with the lid off, you will see, not just one vacant space, but lots of little cells which hold all the acid fluid. If one of these cells gets damaged, the battery will be weakened, but if a few of them are damaged, the battery will be useless. The whole power output of the battery depends on each cell inter-relating functionally.

Our lives are like this. We can think of our lives as having small compartments like finance, home-life, relationships, spirituality, gift, and job, etc. Our lives need to be gathered together in all these areas in order for them to function effectively.

If there are bits of our life that do not function in the way they should and do not relate as they should, then its effectiveness will be wiped out. Some bits may be good, but the bad bits will spoil the lot. For example, we will never make a great preacher, if we never take time to read our Bible and prepare our heart; we will never be a really effective pastor, if our home-life is in a mess; and we will never be able to minister effectively to other people, if our emotions are not gathered together. We need to live disciplined, gathered-together lives, if we ever are going to be really effective for God.

PART 3.4
Spiritual Maturity

The Scriptures make it clear that God's aim for His people is for them to grow into maturity in Him (Ephesians 4:11–16). Maturity is the result of the process of growth in our experience. It results in us becoming more Christ-like and this does not happen overnight (2 Corinthians 3:18).

Some questions to ask ourselves to assess whether we are growing in maturity in Christ include:

- *Can I perceive real growth in my life?*

  - How much have I grown in the last year/in the last two years/in the last five years/in the last ten years?

- *Where have I grown?*

  - In my knowledge of the Scriptures?

  - In my spiritual understanding?

  - In the development of my gifts?

  - In wisdom and discernment?

  - In the eyes of others (do they have a better opinion of me now than they did before)?

  - In confidence?

  - In my understanding of myself?

  - In my understanding of others?

  - In overcoming difficulties?

  - In handling life and circumstances?

  - In coping with pressure?

  - In my relationship with other people?

  - In the development of my ministry?

- *Is the growth I have perceived balanced or is it only in certain areas? What can I do to improve?*

This is a good exercise to be honest about. I have only suggested some areas of growth here; you can add your own to the list. If you find that you have not grown in any area, do not despair, because discovery is the first stage of recovery.

It is alright to feel godly sorrow if you discover no growth in an area, because godly sorrow leads to repentance (2 Corinthians 7:10); but it is wrong to indulge in self-pity which only leads to depression. God wants to restore to all Christians the years in which we have seen destruction rather than growth (Joel 2:25–27).

PART 3.5
Attainment

'Forgetting what is behind and straining toward what is ahead, I press on toward the goal to win the prize for which God has called me heavenward.'

(Philippians 3:13, 14)

Computers cannot predict the future, they can only project into the future using whatever information has been given to them. This is how most human beings live; everything is programmed and they react accordingly. Their future is determined by their past.

Christians, however, do not need to live like this, because the Holy Spirit, who indwells them, can actually take something of God and of tomorrow and transpose it into their lives, so that it determines and helps them in their actions. Christians do not have to live mechanistically, reacting to their circumstances in predetermined ways; they can bring God into the situation and live far more effective, fruitful lives as a result.

Human beings get a tremendous amount of satisfaction when they know they have done something well. God doesn't want us to be motivated just by this or by a competitive, fleshly spirit of attainment, or by the strong desire that most people have to be liked; He wants us to be motivated by love for Him and a desire to obey His will. When we become believers, we need to learn how to achieve things and stay motivated in the Holy Spirit. We are made alive in the Holy Spirit, and we need to live and achieve in the power of the Spirit, instead of in the flesh.

We need to take a good look at the level of attainment in our lives at all sorts of levels. It is unlikely, if we failed to achieve anything at a secular or personal level, that we will ever do so in the spiritual. Christians should excel in whatever they are doing, because they should be doing everything for the glory of God.

Assess the level of achievement in:

- your job
- your relationships
- your personal ambitions
- your ministry

Consider the following questions:

- Do you achieve whatever you set out to achieve?
- If God gives you something to do, do you finish it?
- Does your life consist of one failure after another? If so, why?
- Is it true that spiritual dissatisfaction is bred out of non-achievement?
- Do you always want to move from one job or place to another, because you cannot seem to find satisfaction anywhere? If so, why?

Personal Notes

Personal Notes

Pause for Thought

Take time with this short exercise of assessment and answer the two important questions as far as you are able:

- What factors have prevented achievement in your life?
    - lack of motivation
    - lack of clear goals
    - lack of realistic assessment
    - lack of opportunity
    - lack of support
    - lack of faith
    - lack of training/discipleship
    - lack of encouragement

- What factors have contributed towards anything you have achieved in your life?

'Two men looked out though prison bars; the one saw mud, the other stars.'

As Christians, we must know where we are going in God; and then we must go for it whole-heartedly. When God sets before us an open door, we need to go through it and, in the power of the Holy Spirit, do what God has set before us to do. How many Christians are sitting at the threshold of an open door? How many Christians have not found the door? How many Christians are going down a blind alley?

PART 3.6
Impressions/presentation

W e all create an image in the minds/eyes of other people by how we present ourselves.

The following questions will help you discern how you relate to other people, and what effect they have on you and you have on them.

Answer the questions honestly; and then go through them with your marriage partner or a close friend.

- Is the image you present to other people positive or negative? Is it helpful or does it hinder your work for God?

- Have you ever considered what sort of image you do project and what sort of image you want to project to other people?

- Are you tidy or untidy? Do you think the answer to this question is important? Would you be happy to bring the Lord Jesus Himself into your home, car, office, etc.?

- What is your personal hygiene like, i.e. does it bring glory to God or does it turn people away from God?

- What do you communicate to other people by your body language, i.e. confidence, timidity, brashness, pride, humility, etc.?

- What do your relationships communicate about you? What sort of people surround you? Do you rub off on them? Do they rub off on you? What are these people left with after being with you?

Some Christians need to smarten up and others need to relax. We need to be at ease with ourselves and not try to live up to everybody else's expectation of us. Most importantly, however, we need to bring glory to God in everything we do!

'May the God of peace, who through the blood of the eternal covenant brought back from the dead our Lord Jesus, that great Shepherd of the sheep, equip you with everything good for doing his will, and may he work in us what is pleasing to him, through Jesus Christ, to whom be glory for ever and ever. Amen.'

(Hebrews 13:20, 21)

Assignment: *A Spiritual Review*

N ow that you have studied Section 3, again take some time to complete the following exercise. In one sense this is a very simple exercise, in another it will be deeply searching and, perhaps challenging.

Before you begin ask the Lord to help you to be honest and to give you strength and insight to face the challenge. Jesus does not show us truth to kill us but to set us free.

If, when you have completed the exercise, you feel you need help then discuss the issue with your pastor or trusted Christian friend before you share the results in a group setting.

Let's begin.

1. First, find somewhere to sit quietly and consider your response to the general challenge which has been presented to you by this section. Can you express this challenge in words? If so, write it down.

_____

_____

_____

_____

_____

_____

_____

2. Now: take time to respond to the particular challenges of some of the questions raised by the content of the section.

    For example:

    a) Can I perceive real growth in my life?

        • In the past year _____

        • In the past five years _____

        • In the past ten years _____

    b) In what particular areas have I seen growth take place?

        • Spiritual wisdom _____

        • Scriptural understanding _____

        • Development of gift _____

        • Personal confidence _____

        • Emotional stability _____

        • Relationship with others _____

        • Personal habits _____

        • Ability to cope under pressure _____

        • Personal presentation _____

2. Write a brief description of yourself to yourself:

    _____

    _____

    _____

    _____

    _____

    _____

    _____

    _____

3. What factors or circumstances cause you to react negatively?

_____

_____

_____

_____

_____

_____

_____

_____

_____

Can you describe the effect(s) of this reaction in spiritual, emotional and physical terms?

_____

_____

_____

_____

_____

_____

_____

_____

4. Note the following ratings:

a) Well ordered and fruitful

b) Fairly good, but needs improvement

c) Poorly ordered

d) Not controlled or monitored

Now apply them to assess your discipline and fruitfulness in the following important areas in your life and lifestyle:

☐ relationships with other people

☐ the use of your time

☐ handling finances

☐ emotional stability

☐ home environment

☐ working life

☐ church involvement

☐ personal habits

☐ conversation and use of words

☐ reading the Scriptures

☐ personal prayer life

☐ personal hygiene and dress

☐ development of your mind

☐ deployment of your gifts and talents

☐ use of free time

☐ watching television

5. Finally, complete the following scriptures which will encourage you to be sure of God's continuing help day by day as you determine to grow and develop in every area of your life.

a) Philippians 3:12–14:

'Not that _____ all this,

or have already _____ ,

but I press on to _____

for which Christ Jesus _____ .'

'Forgetting _____ and

straining towards _____ ,

I press on towards the goal _____

_____ for which God has called me heavenward.'

b) Philippians 4:13:

'I can do _____ through him

_____ .'

Answers

Answers to Questions 1–4 of this assignment are personal.

5. See Bible

SECTION 4
Redeeming the Time

Introduction

Key Verses

PART 4.1   God's Timing

PART 4.2   Time Wasters

PART 4.3   Assessing Our Performance

PART 4.4   Ways of Disciplining Our Time

PART 4.5   Sabbath Rest

PART 4.6   Rest and Refreshment

PART 4.7   Creating New Habits

Conclusion

Introduction

This is Your Life!

'Today unused is lost forever, and tomorrow may
never come!' (Ted Engstrom)

T ime can been defined as the measurable period in which
things happen. The time allotted to us by God is continually being used up. It can be used fruitfully and productively
in His service, but only if we, as His servants, are willing.
Unfortunately, most people thoughtlessly squander time. Instead
of being careful how they live each day, the years fly by and
little is achieved. As Christians we should live each day as if
tomorrow were our last (Mark 13:32–37; Matthew 6:34).

As Oswald Sanders once wrote,

'If we are meticulously careful in the use of the days,
the years will take care of themselves.'

As Christians we should approach every day with a sense of awe
and purpose. Here is a stretch of road that we will never pass
again. We must learn how to organise and steward our time so
that our work/life priorities are achieved, namely God's work/
will. This will mean that, at times, we will need to make difficult
decisions about which things to give our time to. After all, we
can only be in one place at a time! A house group leader may
have to refuse an invitation to dinner, a pastor may have
to ignore a television programme, a church elder may have to
neglect a hobby, etc., so that they have the time to do those
things which God wants them to do. We will also have to make
choices between seemingly worthy or important ways to spend
our time, e.g. between two people requiring counselling or
ministry, or between family and church work. If we seek God,
He will make it clear how He wants us to use our time. In fact,
the Counsellor, who leads us into all truth, will show us the most
important call/demand upon our time, if we give Him the room.

Key Verses

Mark 13:32–37

Ephesians 5:15–17

Luke 13:32, 33

Colossians 4:2–6

2 Corinthians 5:9, 10

2 Thessalonians 3:6–13

PART 4.1
God's Timing

'Today is unique! It has never occurred before and it will never be repeated. At midnight it will end, quietly, suddenly, totally. Forever! But the hours between now and then are opportunities with eternal possibilities. You will never again worship your Lord or share His love with someone today. With His enablement, live this day to the full – as if it were your last day on earth. It may be!' (Charles Swindoll)

We need to remember that everything happens according to God's plans and timing. We might want everything done in a hurry (or even yesterday!), but God may have other ideas. It is God whom we are serving primarily, not goals or even people. We need to wait upon Him, do what He asks us to do for Him, and then trust Him with the timing.

Once we know our task in God, we can measure our use of time against that task. Being busy just for the sake of it, even in our work for the Lord, is counter-productive and demotivating. We need to establish life and time-use priorities that are derived from God's word to us and from the call He places on our lives.

Discovering the will of God for our lives and living in the good of it on a day to day basis should be the lifestyle of every Christian. This is the way that Jesus lived and we are to follow His example (John 5:19; 1 John 2:6). He knew that He was working according to His Father's plan; a plan that embraced every hour and made provision for every contingency. He did everything well and nothing remained incomplete due to lack of time or spoiled due to undue haste. In fact, He managed to complete all the work God had given Him to do in the 24 hours a day given to all mankind (John 17:4), because He lived according to the divine timetable for His life (Luke 2:49; 13:32, 33). As Christians, we need to do the same.

Remember, God's work is the most important thing that we can do. After all, the work we do for God will last long after everything else. We, therefore, need to learn how to determine the difference between what needs to be done in God and what we would like to do. Remember also, there will always be enough time to do God's will. After all, He has created time and He has planned our good works in advance (Ephesians 2:10). We will never be short of time, as long as we do not waste this precious, non-repeatable resource, and we fit in with God's plans and purposes for our life.

> *'Be very careful, then, how you live – not as unwise but as wise, making the most of every opportunity (redeeming the time,* AV; *make the best use of your time,* J.B. Phillips), *because the days are evil.'*
>
> (Ephesians 5:15, 16)

PART 4.2
Time Wasters

I n all our lives there are elements and factors which detract from the proper and most fruitful use of our time.

- *Indecision* – Decisions have to be made and often these will involve an element of risk. We need to accept the risks and get on and make the decisions required, in the best way we can. Procrastination (or the putting off or delaying of action) is one of the chief thieves of time and, unfortunately, it is a common fault of many of us. In fact, many of the items which have become bugbears in our lives are those things which are put off until another day.

- *Lack of planning* – Many of God's servants are never quite sure what they should be doing. It is helpful to write a list of the things that have to be done and to rank them in order of importance. Then plan your day/week/month/year making sure that the things that are priorities for that day/week/month/year are done during times when we can give them our best.

- *Lack of organisation* – Can you never find what you want, when you want it? Is your desk or even your whole office such a mess that you cannot concentrate on what you are doing? Get organised and get a good filing system. The time invested in getting one together may save you many hours later. Also, make sure your desk is tidy and you can only see that which you are working on at the time.

- *Indiscipline* – Time can be so easily wasted simply because we do not get on and do the things that need to be done. Instead, we dream, have yet another cup of coffee, push the paper on our desk around, talk to yet another person about how their holiday or weekend went, etc. Undisciplined time tends to be used up doing the things we are not very good at; controlled by loud, strong, domineering people; governed by the tyranny of the immediate or urgent; given to things that appeal to our flesh; and invested in things that bring public acclaim and immediate reward.

- *Doing too much* – This will often cause us to achieve less and to do the things that we are doing less well. If your work load is too great, lessen it by giving out the jobs that can be delegated. Remember also to say 'No' when you need to, and to put off the routine and trivial until times when you are less sharp/active in the day.

- *Being busy doing nothing* – Too often we do things because they have always been done or because we like the appearance of being busy, when in reality we are achieving very little of value. God's servants should ask Him what He wants them to do. Activities should never be there for their own sake, but rather for the sake of getting God's work done in His way and time.

- *Laziness* – Our flesh often likes to take it easy. In fact, it likes to be pandered to and given in to. We need to make sure that we do not do this. The work of God is too important for us to be lazy in our attitude to it. God has entrusted us with His will and it is our responsibility in Him to carry this out faithfully and to the best of our ability (Matthew 25:14–30; 2 Thessalonians 3:6–15).

- *Lack of stickability* – God's people need stickability. They need to emulate the attitude of Jesus with regard to the work of God. He said, *'My food is to do the will of Him who sent me and to finish His work'* (John 4:34). Many people get swamped by the things they have half-done or shelved. In fact, they often get so weighed down with these things that they give up and end up doing nothing. God wants us to go on and to complete that which we have been given by Him to do (1 Corinthians 9:24–27; Philippians 3:12–14).

- *Panic* – This can happen when our difficulties and problems get too much for us and they overwhelm us. The problem here is often simply that we hyperventilate (i.e. breathe too quickly and so become light-headed). What we should do in this case is to stop, relax and take slow deep breaths (i.e. get the oxygen out of our system). Once we have begun to calm down, we should pray and bring the situation to God and realise that in Him we can do all things (Philippians 4:13). Trying to do anything when we are panicking is a waste of time. It would be far better to stop work until we regain our composure in God.

- *Interruptions* – Have you noticed how often the telephone or front door bell rings when you are doing something that is important or which needs to be done urgently? It is helpful to set aside times in a day in which you can work undisturbed. This may mean putting the answer-phone on or even taking the 'phone off the hook. Visitors should also be screened, when possible, and given appointment times that are convenient to you. Another person's emergency may not be as important as they think, so do not readily make exceptions even for emergencies. It may also be helpful to see people over lunch, or at times during the day when interruptions will not affect you. Remember though, even unexpected interruptions may be caused by God.

- *Meetings* – Too many of God's leaders waste vast amounts of time going to meetings that they do not need to attend. Church leaders do not usually have to be at every church meeting, attend every conference, or go to all the local fraternal meetings. God's leaders need to work out their priorities and only go to the meetings that they need to in Him.

- *Afternoon lethargy* – Staring into space or letting our mind wander as we enjoy the pleasant feeling of a full stomach after a particularly good lunch does not get the work done. Some simple helps to avoiding afternoon lethargy include: eating a light lunch; not having the office too hot; and saving the jobs that excite us until after lunch (in order to help get us re-motivated for work).

- *TV/radio/reading/telephone* – These can be useful tools which we can use in order to relax and even to edify our minds, but we need to be careful. Too many people waste much of their life because of these things. We need to do God's work first and fit these things in around what He wants us to do for Him.

There are probably many other time wasters that you could think of which cause you as an individual to waste time. Do not put up with these, but rather try and do something about them. We only have one life to live for God, so let's make the best use of it!

PART 4.3
Assessing Our Performance

'Time can be lost, but it can never be retrieved. It cannot be hoarded, it must be spent. Nor can it be postponed. If it is not used productively, it is irretrievably lost.'
(J. Oswald Sanders)

i) Effective use of time

Peter Drucker has devised three diagnostic questions to assess the effectiveness of time management in an organisation. These are:

- What am I doing that really does not need to be done by me or anyone else?

- Which of the activities on my time log could be handled by someone else as well if not better?

- What do I do that wastes the time of other people?

Although these questions are primarily aimed at business management, there is some value in answering them ourselves. It is a good idea to sit down and work out how every half hour of your waking day is used. Ask questions like:

- Is this activity productive in my service for God?

- Does this activity contribute anything meaningful to my life/family/church?

- Do I need to be doing this?

Most of us will find that we do not use our time at all well and that there are simple things we could do to improve in this area.

ii) Peak time function

Every person would also benefit from finding out when they function at their peak during a day. This will vary from person to person and will also vary in an individual's life according to circumstances.

The easiest way to do this is to assess at the end of the day when you did your most productive work during that day (only you will know this!). This needs to be assessed during more normal periods of life and over an extended period of time, i.e. for at least a few weeks. Our most effective/productive times could be after a nap, in the morning, after lunch, after a stimulating conversation, etc.

Once you have worked out when you function best in a day and week, you should timetable into these times the really important tasks, i.e. those which require you to be functioning at top level in mind and body in order for them to be completed quickly, efficiently and successfully.

PART 4.4
Ways of Disciplining Our Time

- *Knowing ourselves*, i.e. when (and why) we work at our best, so that we can choose the best times and conditions in which to do our God-given tasks. We then need to develop our life/work programme around this. We must also re-evaluate this with God regularly, because things do change and we should continually want to use our time fruitfully and stay on course with God.

- *Ranking jobs* in order of priority/importance and doing the most important ones first (when possible). This will save us a lot of emotional energy (because we will not have to worry about doing the job for as long) and it will usually save us some time. People cannot afford to concentrate their efforts and invest their time in things of secondary importance, when the primary things are shouting for attention. Every Christian should plan their days carefully and choose to release their time to the things which are the most important time-use priorities.

- *Organising our time into blocks* can be a help to enable us to manage our time more efficiently. For example, we can split the day into morning, afternoon and evening and decide what we will do in each. To do this effectively, we will need a watch, a diary, a notebook, and a pen which we carry around with us always.

- *Keep a regular routine* – Set aside a certain block of time on the same day each week for a certain job, e.g. sermon preparation, visitation, group study, and even time given to the family, etc.

- *Plan well in advance* – This will enable us to have the space in our busy schedules to fit in the really important priorities of our time. We can then let all the other demands on our time flow around our priorities. A well organised personal diary will be essential to do this. A wise person will also know how to look ahead and see the places which are going to be the most personally challenging, i.e. where tiredness and loss of motivation are likely to occur. That person will then plan how to gather the necessary energy and motivation ahead of the time it is needed, and know how to parcel it out in order to see them through these times. It is alright to trust in God, but He wants us to look ahead in Him and to draw on Him for the difficulties He shows us are to come. He also wants us to stay prepared in Him for anything that may come our way (Hebrews 12:1–3; Ephesians 6:10–18; 2 Timothy 4:2; 1 Peter 5:8, 9). We, therefore, need to make sure that we are meeting with Him and drawing from Him on a daily basis.

- *Be an early starter* – Much can be achieved first thing in a day, because our personal efficiency is highest during the first few hours after a night's sleep, and there tend to be less interruptions. Also, do not take 20 minutes to get out of bed, but rather wake yourself up quickly by getting washed, dressed and going. Someone once said, 'If we sleep less, we live more.' In fact, if we sleep for one hour less per day, we add well over two years of waking time to our life.

- *We should concentrate on what we are doing* (Colossians 3:23) – Even a short time of doing this is worth many hours of half-hearted attention!

- *Do it now!* – We should never let the things that we have to do mount up so high that we get swamped by them.

PART 4.5
Sabbath Rest

- Sabbath rest may be defined as a time where our normal work and leisure practices are stopped and we set aside a period of time to refresh ourselves in the Lord. It is not a legal requirement that we have to observe for a day once a week, but rather is something that a mature Christian should live in the good of many times a day.

- Sabbath rest periods should be a time-use priority in the life of every Christian. All God's people need to spend quality time with Him, resting in Him and drawing from Him. This is the rest that we really need if we are going to be fruitful for God. What the world calls rest is really just amusement or leisure.

  Of course, these things do have some value, because they enable friendships, exercise our body, relieve stress, stimulate our mind, provide a change, etc., but they do not do anything to help us spiritually. The rest in God that we need, and which is the most important key to effective Christian service, is giving God the opportunity to meet with us and build us up spiritually.

  If this foundation of our life is not well laid, we will be unable to stand our ground in God. Remember, God wants us to be able to do any work He asks us to do for Him, no matter what confronts us. It is not what we do, but who we are in God that counts.

- God showed us the need for rest by building it into His created order. At the end of each of the days of the creation story, God rested and evaluated what He had done; then, on the final day, He rested for the entire day. He blessed that day and made it holy, because He rested from all the work of creation that He had done and He refreshed Himself (Genesis 2:2, 3). God later insisted on the children of Israel having a rest day when they first came out of Egypt by not only commanding it (Exodus 20:8–11; 31:12–17), but also by only providing food on six days of the week (Exodus 16:1–35). Hebrews 4:1–11 explains that there is a Sabbath rest for the people of God that we should make every effort to enter into. Christians can live constantly in the rest of God by abiding in Christ and living in His peace.

- God created us with a need to rest and meet with Him. To ignore this is to try and live a Christian life without plugging into our Source. The result will be spiritual bankruptcy and emptiness. Every Christian needs to make room in their lives on a daily basis for times of Sabbath rest in which they meet with God and make room for Him to work on and speak into their lives. This is best built into a day's beginning, because it will then prepare and enable us in our service for God throughout the rest of that day. However, these times should not be restricted to a set time every day. In fact, every Christian should be having times of Sabbath rest many times a day when they need it. Note, a Sabbath rest is more than what many evangelical Christians call their 'quiet time'. These tend to be reduced to merely a mindless, over-organised routine.

⇨ **This Sabbath rest principle:**

- *stops the workaholic*

- *encourages discipline of life*

- *gets our eyes back on the Lord and gives us time to get our lives back into godly perspective*

- *helps prevent excessive, imbalanced living*

- *gives us time to evaluate with God what we have been doing with our lives over recent times*

- *makes room in our lives to establish our intentions of living a Christ-centred tomorrow*

'Seek first his kingdom and his righteousness, and all these things will be given to you as well.'

(Matthew 6:33)

PART 4.6
Rest and Refreshment

We all need to work hard and give our best to that work, but we are not machines. We need to have periods of rest and relaxation built into our day, week and year. Pushing ourselves too hard, in the end, only reduces our effectiveness and so is counter-productive.

R & R times can range from just five minutes in the midst of a pressure-filled day, to having a long holiday. Stress build up is cumulative, i.e. it keeps building with each pressure event that takes place in our life. If we do not reduce this stress, it continues to build up until it starts causing us to be irritable, have a pre-occupied mind, or manifest other bodily symptoms like muscle tension, headaches, heart trouble, etc. Stress even pushes many people to drugs or alcohol in order to seek some relief from it. We need to build into each day, times in which we relax, stretch and breathe deeply, push aside the cause of our stress, and stop thinking about our work and our problems.

PART 4.7
Creating New Habits

If you decide that you are not organising your time in the most effective way and you want/need to change, then remember that it does take time to develop new habits (i.e. for patterns of behaviour to become second nature). In fact, it takes up to a month (and sometimes even longer) to transform a new way of behaving into a comfortable habit. Unfortunately, most people do not realise this and so they give up trying to change after a week or so. The other mistake that people make is trying to introduce too wide-ranging or dramatic changes. People who attempt to do this often find it is unbearable after a time and, therefore, they revert back to their old, comfortable habits.

The key to making lasting changes in our behaviour is to make any necessary changes gradually, smoothly and systematically, and persist until those changes become part of our normal routine. Of course, at times, God will want to do a radical work in our lives which will cause us to change dramatically in a very short time. These changes are worked in us by the Holy Spirit and we are enabled to persist in them by Him. However, it must never be forgotten that usually God expects us to change ourselves simply by disciplining our lives. In fact, the Scriptures are full of moral imperatives which ask us to do certain things in order to live life as God intends. He will give us the strength and enabling we need in order to do this, but first we must use our will and decide to make a conscious effort to change.

Some other helpful tips for use when attempting to create a new habit include:

- *Do not overload yourself.* Only take on what you can handle or what God has shown you that you need to be doing.

- *Write it down.* Then you can see and remember what you decided to do. Do not try to keep it in your head alone, because ideas kept there tend to be vague/unspecific and, therefore, less able to be applied successfully to life.

- *Tell someone else what you are doing.* They can encourage you and hold you accountable to your decision to change.

- *Start the process of change immediately.* Otherwise, like many of our good intentions, it will be put off until tomorrow! Never wait until you feel like changing, because you will probably be waiting for a long time.

- *Continue to practice or work at your new behaviour/habit until it becomes second nature to you.* Once you reach a point where you automatically exhibit the desired behaviour, you can relax a bit.

Conclusion

T ime is a God-given gift which needs to be invested carefully by us in God's future. Remember, we are stewards for God of our time and we will be held accountable for how we used it (Romans 14:12; 2 Corinthians 5:10). It is a tragedy that so many Christians look back on the way they have used their time with regret.

To avoid this, every Christian should sit down and look at the way they use their time and try to make the best use of it they can for God. We need to understand what God wants us to do with our life at any particular moment (if you do not know, then ask Him!). We should be people who hold spiritual dynamite within us which we make available for God to use. He will discharge this through us, if we do His work in His time and way.

> 'We are always complaining that our days are few and acting as though there would be no end of them.'
> (Seneca)

> *'Teach us to number our days aright, that we may gain a heart of wisdom.'* (Psalm 90:12)

SECTION 5
Waiting on God

Introduction

The greatest need

Effective spiritual life begins and ends with a full dependence on God. In fact, every Christian needs the Holy Spirit to work in and through him constantly in order to do the work of God. We always need to be making room for God in our lives and we need to be waiting on Him regularly.

Too many Christians relegate waiting on God to times of stress and difficulty. Others try everything but waiting on God in order to find fulfilment in life. These people try to stay motivated as Christians and attempt to fill the void in their life by going through the right activities, but they find it does not work and they are, therefore, tempted to abandon their commitment to God. God is more concerned about our availability to Him, than He is with our ability or our work for Him. We can do nothing that matters for eternity without God.

All God's servants should be people who meet with God regularly. This will help them to keep Jesus as Lord of all their lives; help them to live humbly before their Almighty God who they are progressively getting to know; enable them to worship Him to whom they owe everything they are and have; and help them to live holy lives which do not dishonour God, thus enabling them to stay as pure vessels which God can use whenever He needs.

Key Verses

Psalm 63:1–8

Luke 10:38–42

1 Corinthians 2:9–16

Hebrews 10:19–22

James 1:5–8

PART 5.1
The Need to Wait on God

The Bible states that living a Christian life is not going to be easy. In fact, it suggests that we weigh up the cost before we start (Luke 14:25–35), because we are going to undergo trials, persecutions, suffering and difficulty. The only way to live such a life is to draw on the resources of God. They are available to all who need them, but we often need to wait on God to receive them.

Waiting on God is not a one-off thing, but needs to be a daily discipline that spans our life-time. It needs to be something we incorporate into our lifestyle, because otherwise we will not be able to cope with normal life as a Christian, let alone when the difficult times come. Many Christians feel that their lives are too busy to give the necessary time to this activity, so they rarely, if ever, do it. No Christian can afford to do this. It is a sure recipe for disaster. If even the Son of God, Jesus, needed to spend time with God in order to carry out His work on earth, how much more do we as His followers need to do the same. God has made a way for us to come into His very presence through Jesus and He wants us to avail ourselves of this tremendous privilege (Ephesians 2:18; 3:12; Hebrews 4:16; 10:19–22; 1 John 3:21, 22). God wants us to come to Him and to develop our relationship with Him.

> *'Come near to God and he will come near to you.'*
> (James 4:8)

Many Christians know how they should be living, but as they look at themselves they find that all is not in order. They know the ideals, but they do not seem to be able to live up to them. It is only as we see ourselves as God sees us and we again yield our lives to Him that things begin to look better. We should let Him point out the problems, give us His strategy for living, give us His heart and His love, and in-fill us with the power we need to carry out His work. This does not just happen. God has reserved such provision to those who wait on Him (Matthew 6:25–34).

PART 5.2
A Question of Priorities

Christians cannot function effectively for God unless their lives are right with Him. In fact, Christianity will not seem to work unless our inner spiritual life is in order. Therefore, waiting on God needs to be our number one priority of life as a Christian.

Most people spend the majority of their time and energy attaining possessions, position, achievements, friends or a good family life etc. Of course, all these uses of our time are valid, but as Christians they should not be our first priority.

Jesus said the greatest commandment was to love the Lord your God with all your heart, soul, strength and mind (Luke 10:27) and you can only do this if you know God first. He is willing to come and to reveal Himself to us and meet with us, if we make room in our busy lives to meet with Him.

If Christians could look at their time-use priorities with God's eyes, they probably would be shocked. Remember Jesus' words to Martha who was very busy serving Him and complaining that her sister Mary was doing nothing to help. He said Mary chose the better thing because she sat at His feet and was listening to Him (Luke 10:38–42).

Most Christians are weaker than they should be spiritually because they do not give the time they need to wait on God. We need to see our time as God sees it and use it wisely, having His priorities for its use.

In the modern world, where competition is encouraged and where achievement and the making of money are the hallmarks of success, we find that there is a strong pressure to push aside the things God asks us to do. These things are seen as unimportant and do not demand our attention as much as our family, friends and those with whom we work. These all have a voice which can scream at us, whereas God wants us to choose to come to Him.

PART 5.3
God's Order

G od created us to work from our spirit and heart outwards (John 7:37–39; Luke 6:43–45; Matthew 15:18, 19). If our heart (which can be thought of as the doorway to our spirit) is in a disordered state, we can expect nothing but turmoil to surface.

Most Christians have learned to cover this up very well, but it renders them largely ineffective for God. It is only when we are right with God in heart that God can begin to use us by His Holy Spirit to touch the lives of other people.

Our heart is made right by waiting on God and responding to anything of which the Holy Spirit is convicting us. Once we have repented, we can make Jesus Lord again of all our life. We can keep our hearts right by allowing the peace of God to reign there (Philippians 4:7; Colossians 3:15), by obeying our consciences, by disciplining our lives so that we spend time each day waiting on God, by making sure we filter the things we allow ourselves to participate in, and by doing that which God wants us to do (Psalms 51:10–12; 139:23, 24).

> *'Above all else, guard your heart, for it is the wellspring
> of life.'*   (Proverbs 4:23)

As Christians we should so know God that we need nothing else in order to stand firm in Him. We should be able to go on in

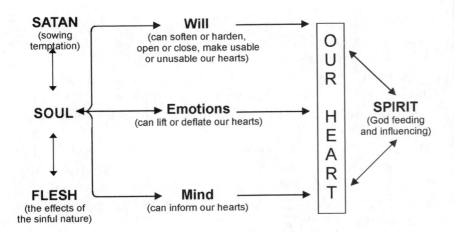

God no matter what is happening around us. Nothing should be able to shake us or cause us to fail or give up. We can only do this by offering ourselves to God and allowing Him to change us so that we become more Christ-like (Romans 12:1, 2; Ephesians 4:22–24; 2 Corinthians 3:18; Philippians 2:12, 13).

We also need to yield our lives to the Holy Spirit who can show us God and lead us in His ways (1 Corinthians 2:10–16). For many Christians, this process has all but stopped. The reason is that they do not yield every area of their life over to God and, therefore, He cannot work through those areas. These things clutter up these people's lives so much that the Holy Spirit is hindered in His ability to flow through them. This may happen to such an extent that it seems God cannot use them. As Christians, we have been created to have living water flow from within us and, if this is not our normal experience, something is wrong.

Waiting on God is not an option. It should not be the domain of the more spiritually minded only. In fact, it is an essential part of every believer's life. Seeking God in solitude and silence is not a lazy alternative to doing something more fruitful for God nor is it unproductive, but rather it is the foundation upon which we should build our lives and our service for God.

PART 5.4
We Need to Let God Have Control

Unfortunately, in many Christian lives the Holy Spirit has to spend all His time sorting them out, instead of being able to empower them in their service for God. These people often think of themselves as not spiritual enough for God and, therefore, they make no attempt to get right with Him. They simply put up with their problems and let others do all the work.

This is not God's way. Instead of having a life in which God is enthroned and in total control, they live a life that is partly controlled by God, partly by themselves and partly by the enemy. This acts like a cork or log-jam and makes these people's lives ineffective for God.

Even if such people do decide to serve the Lord, they usually quickly find that they do not have what it takes or they fail to match up to the standards and expectations which God has for them (or they have for themselves). They, therefore, run out of steam and give up.

It is out of a believer's relationship with God that they grow in their ministry. God knows where we are at and what we need to know at any particular time. We need to make room in our lives for God to be able to reveal His truths and will when it is needed. God will prompt us to come to Him, but He will not force us.

We need to respond with a willing heart and make ourselves available to Him. We need to learn how to respond to God's Spirit whenever He speaks to us and be able to draw aside at any time to listen to Him. The Lord wants His servants to always be dependent on Him and His resources and never to rely purely on their own strength and ability. If a servant can maintain such a walk with God, it will save them much wasted time.

PART 5.5
Deep Calls to Deep

Pause and take a moment to read Psalm 42 from *The Message*:

> '*A white-tailed deer drinks*
>   *from the creek;*
> *I want to drink God,*
> *Deep draughts of God.*
> *I'm thirsty for God-alive.*
> *I wonder, "Will I ever make it –*
>   *arrive and drink in God's presence?"*
> *I'm on a diet of tears –*
>   *tears for breakfast, tears for supper.*
> *All day long*
>   *people knock at my door,*
> *Pestering,*
>   *"Where is this God of yours?"*
> *These are the things I go over and over,*
>   *emptying out the pockets of my life.*

I was always at the head of the worshipping crowd,
    right out in front.
Leading them all,
    eager to arrive and worship,
Shouting praises, singing thanksgiving –
    celebrating, all of us, God's feast!
Why are you down in the dumps, dear soul?
    Why are you crying the blues?
Fix my eyes on God –
    Soon I'll be praising again.
He puts a smile on my face.
    He's my God.

When my soul is in the dumps, I rehearse
    everything I know of you,
From Jordan depths to Hermon heights,
    including Mount Mizar.
Chaos calls to chaos,
    to the tune of whitewater rapids.
Your breaking surf, your thundering breakers
    crash and crush me.
Then Yahweh promises to love me all day,
    sing songs through the night!
    My life is God's prayer.

Sometimes I ask God, my rock-solid God,
    "Why did you let me down?
Why am I walking around in tears,
    harassed by my enemies?"
They're out for the kill, these
    tormentors with their obscenities,
Taunting day after day,
    "Where is this God of yours?"

Why are you down in the dumps, dear soul?
    Why are you crying the blues?
Fix my eyes on God –
    soon I'll be praising again.
He puts a smile on my face.
    He's my God.'

This Psalm expresses the desperation of a man to meet with God. He had found the reality of spiritual depth with God and he needed to meet with God afresh. As Christians, we all need to learn how to reach into the depths of our own being and into the depths of the heart of God.

Waiting on God is like those people who absail into deep underground caverns. The people who really know what they are doing, know how to get safely right into the depths, where no person has gone before.

Most of us have a mechanistic approach to our religion. We read someone's book or we get someone's ideas and we try to programme these things into our lives. Christianity should be deeper than this. Whilst theology, doctrine, practical and strategic things are important and interesting, they should not ultimately form the foundation of our faith in God.

There is a deeper reality of God, something which it is hard to define. The Psalmist here was searching after this as a deer pants for water. This is a searching of the soul after God, an openness of the heart to God, a God-awareness in our spirit that really, in the end, you cannot teach other people about.

When all is said and done, it is only the reality of God which will last for eternity. He is the ultimate reality. Our experience, ministry, vision, doctrine etc. will fail, but God will go on for all time. This is where invisible realities are more important and powerful than visible ones. The sense of God is a very real thing, although it is not always immediately touchable or practical. Saying our prayers, sitting quietly, writing things, meditating etc., all need to be an expression of something deeper.

PART 5.6
The Place of Waiting

The Bible talks about the knowledge of God. This is not knowing about God or the externals of religion: it is knowing God Himself!

> *'My ears had heard of you, but now my eyes have seen you.'* (Job 42:5)

The Bible does say that no man shall see God and live (Exodus 33:20), but there is a powerful strand of biblical witness that shows there are people who have seen God and have had dramatically changed lives as a result.

These two statements do not contradict each other, because the former is talking about seeing God with our physical eyes. No man can see God in this way and live. Moses was only able to see God's back, because to look on His face with the naked eye would have been the end of him. We can, however, see God with our spiritual eyes. Isaiah, Ezekiel and John, to name a few, had this kind of experience. They were 'in the spirit' and they saw God; and they were not the same afterwards.

They had such a sense, or understanding, of the living God that it changed who they were. It impinged upon their humanity in an irrevocable way so that God became part of the very fibre of their whole life. We can know something of this ourselves if we give all we are over to God and we make room in our lives in order to meet with Him.

Knowing this sense of God is what counts. It makes us strong and unshakeable. It cannot be destroyed by persecution, disappointment or hardship, whereas, there are many Christians today who would fall apart if they did not get the external trappings of Christianity. In a sense, they have married their religion to the externals, instead of to God Himself.

> *'O God, you are my God, earnestly I seek you; my soul thirsts for you, my body longs for you, in a dry and weary land where there is no water. I have seen you in*

the sanctuary and beheld your power and your glory. Because your love is better than life, my lips will glorify you. I will praise you as long as I live, and in your name I will lift up my hands. My soul will be satisfied as with the richest of foods; with singing lips my mouth will praise you. On my bed I remember you; I think of you through the watches of the night. Because you are my help, I sing in the shadow of your wings. I stay close to you; your right hand upholds me.' (Psalm 63:1–8)

We, like King David, need to know that we can afford to lose our material possessions and our position, but we cannot afford to live without an intimate relationship with God. No matter how bad it got, David knew that his priority was to keep a right relationship with Him. David, like us, was only in real trouble when his relationship with God faltered.

PART 5.7
The Process of Waiting

Waiting on God should not be a mystical, dreamy sort of thing. God is portrayed in the Bible as a vibrant, powerful, real, active, dynamic personality. Meeting with Him should have an effect on our lives. It should be revelation to us; it should make us more aware of God and His ways; it should enable us to grow in understanding and practical wisdom; and it should change our hearts. We can never have this by just reading a couple of books, even if one is the Bible. Many people read, live in, and even worship the Bible, but they hardly know God.

Waiting on God grows out of two polar experiences, and yet in the heart of God they find a conjunction. The *one pole* is God making Himself so real to us that the desire to meet with Him will not go away (Psalm 42:1). The *other pole* is a desperate sense of our need to meet with God in a deep, life-changing way.

PART 5.8
The Practice of Waiting

Some practical tips to enable us to wait on God include:

i) Laying aside

- distractions
- temptations
- concerns (1 Peter 5:7)

We need to seek God for Himself. To aid this, it is helpful to find a place to wait on God which will be free from interruption and interference. It is, therefore, best to be alone when possible.

We must also make sure that our lives are right with God. There is no need to dig around inside ourselves to find this out, because the Holy Spirit will point out anything that needs sorting out when we first come to wait on God.

Sin is like a darkness within us; when we come to God's holiness, that darkness is exposed by God's light. We need to be holy in order to see the Lord (Hebrews 12:14) and we can only achieve this by confessing our sin, repenting and availing ourselves of the redemptive work of Jesus Christ (1 John 1:7, 9).

ii) Taking time (making space)

Allocate time in your programme to wait on God on a regular basis. Be ruthless and do not let excuses or busyness rule the roost. Waiting on the Lord can be done anywhere and at any time, because it is simply a setting aside of our time and our heart in order to seek the Lord and bring Him into our situation. It can be done for a few minutes when needed or it can be carried out over a whole day or even longer. At times, it is valid to go to a quiet retreat where we can set aside a longer period of time in order to wait on the Lord.

Personal Notes

It is best to wait on God first thing in the day. This helps us to be more God-aware during the day; it helps prevent us pushing this important activity into the background; it enables us to start the day right with Him; it allows us to get His order and direction for the day; it invites Him to be in control of our lives; and it assures us that He will look after us etc.

It is also helpful to pray with your family after your private time with God. This helps to keep the Lord central in your family life; it brings unity to the family and a sense of God's peace; and it enables Him to minister where and when needed into your family life. If a servant's personal or family life is not in order, he will not be able to minister to other people effectively.

iii) Training the mind

- concentrate

- meditate

When we first start to wait on God, our minds probably will try to mutiny. We need to discipline ourselves to this and our minds will come around as it becomes a habit and as we start to see results.

We must learn to sound-proof our hearts against the intrusive noises from the world around us, including those demands on our time that scream at us on a regular basis. Many people are so addicted to noise that they find silence louder than noise and so feel very uncomfortable when trying to be quiet. This needs to be overcome if we are ever going to get anywhere in our times of waiting on the Lord.

It is helpful to write down God's words to us so that we do not forget them. We can then obey God to the letter; we will have a record that we can later go to for encouragement and strengthening; we can more readily trace God's hand upon our lives (i.e. see how we have grown in God and how He has proved faithful over the years); and we are helped to externalise, define and make sense of what is happening inside of us.

iv) Finding the right environment

Waiting on God is not dependent on ethos or atmosphere, but finding the environment that best suits us can help us to get into the right frame of mind to meet with the Lord. Find a place/situation in which your spirit can be at ease. It often helps to go to the same place for your times of waiting on the Lord and to consecrate those places to Him. Do not allow these places to be used for anything ungodly. This can help you to settle quickly and get into the right attitude of heart to seek the Lord.

v) Cultivating your spirit (learning how to activate your spirit)

Use:

- quiet (still yourself and relax)
- praise
- thanksgiving
- remembering God's past faithfulness
- worship
- speaking in tongues
- other gifts of the Spirit
- God's Word
- prayer
- reading and meditating on Scripture
- reading good devotional aids (e.g. Oswald Chambers, the *Daily Light*, etc.)
- a change in routine (to shake yourself from lethargy)

Learn to recognise what stimulates your heart towards God. Do not, however, wait for an urge to spend time with Him. Start it as a discipline and let God inspire you and change your attitude. If you have continuing trouble, pray about it with other Christians.

There is a sense in which the person who has met with God is never satisfied. They always want more and they always seem to be panting after God.

Bible Study: *The Heart of the Matter*

> *'Above all else, guard your heart for it is the wellspring of life.'* (Proverbs 4:23)

Heart is one of the most interesting words in the Bible. It occurs a great number of times in many different contexts. It is interesting because, although on occasions it literally means the physical organ, it most often is used to speak of the whole range of human personality, intuition and feeling. This is why the appeal of God is always to the heart:

> *'My son give me your heart.'* (Proverbs 23:26)

God's desire is to reach into the very depths of our being and affect the widest ranges of our experience. When we wait on the Lord it is to the heart that He speaks and it is in our hearts that we know Him most intimately.

1. **Five important areas**

   There are five major areas of life which are encompassed by the term *heart* in the Bible. These can be categorised as:

   1) physical organ
   2) intellectual – mind and thought
   3) the area of our will – decision
   4) emotional – feelings and affections
   5) moral and spiritual life

   Here are 20 scriptures. Look at them and decide which category they fall into. Write the appropriate category beside the right verse.

   ☐ 2 Samuel 18:14   ☐ Psalm 139:23

   ☐ Psalm 81:12   ☐ Proverbs 12:25

   ☐ Matthew 15, 18, 19 ☐ Genesis 6:5

   ☐ Psalm 4:7   ☐ Job 37:1

   ☐ 1 John 3:19, 20   ☐ Psalm 38:10

   ☐ 2 Corinthians 9:7   ☐ Ecclesiastes 2:1

☐ Mark 12:30   ☐ Isaiah 6:10

☐ Psalm 51:10   ☐ James 3:14

☐ Romans 6:17   ☐ Jeremiah 17:9

☐ Psalm 102:4   ☐ 1 Samuel 25:37

2. **The book of Proverbs**

This book speaks a great deal about the heart and the effect on us of what happens there. The following scriptures show us the positive and negative results of what happens through the heart. Complete the texts:

a) Proverbs 12:25:

'An _____ weighs a man down.'

b) Proverbs 13:12:

'Hope _____ makes the _____.'

c) Proverbs 14:10:

'Each heart knows its own _____'

d) Proverbs 14:30:

'A heart at _____ gives _____'

e) Proverbs 15:13:

'A _____ makes the face _____'

f) Proverbs 15:15:

'The _____ heart has a continual _____'

g) Proverbs 16:23:

'A wise man's heart _____'

h) Proverbs 17:20:

'A man of a _____ does not _____'

i) Proverbs 17:22:

'A _____ is good _____'

j) Proverbs 18:15:

'The heart of the _____ acquires _____'

3. **The effect of sin**

    Our heart was made for the love of God and to worship God. Sin dealt a fatal blow to man's heart. Instead of being the crucible within which God could work freely it became the source of everything that is against God.

    Write Jeremiah 17:9

    _____

    _____

    _____

    Write Matthew 15:19

    _____

    _____

    _____

    These scriptures show us that as far as God is concerned defilement comes from within rather than from without.

4. **God's heart surgery**

    Because, as we have seen the heart is the root of the problem, it is also the place where God concentrates His efforts to save and change us. What do the following scriptures tell us about God's work in the heart?

    -   Romans 2:15 _____

        _____

    -   Matthew 13:19 _____

        _____

    -   Ezekiel 11:19 _____

        _____

    -   Romans 10:10 _____

        _____

    -   Romans 5:5 _____

        _____

5. **The response of faith**

God wants us to open our hearts, that is, our whole being to Him. There is nothing in us which He cannot deal with or overcome. Fill in the blanks from 1 John 3:20:

'God is _____ *than* _____

_____ *.'*

a) *His invitation*: Proverbs 23:26

_____

b) *Our response*: Psalm 139:23

_____

c) *Our prayer*: Psalm 51:10

_____

6. **God's promises**

The Scriptures bring us great promises from God. He wants to renew and restore us in our inner being. As we wait in His presence He releases fresh stores of energy and hope into our hearts. Match the following scriptures with the correct promise.

a) ☐ Romans 5:5   1) strengthen

b) ☐ Ephesians 3:17   2) guard

c) ☐ Philippians 4:7   3) encourage

d) ☐ 1 Thessalonians 3:13   4) dwell

e) ☐ 2 Thessalonians 2:17   5) direct

f) ☐ 2 Thessalonians 3:5   6) love

Answers

1.
[1]	2 Samuel 18:14	[2]	Psalm 139:23
[3]	Psalm 81:12	[4]	Proverbs 12:25
[2]	Matthew 15, 18, 19	[5]	Genesis 6:5
[4]	Psalm 4:7	[1]	Job 37:1
[5]	1 John 3:19, 20	[1]	Psalm 38:10
[3]	2 Corinthians 9:7	[2]	Ecclesiastes 2:1
[4]	Mark 12:30	[2]	Isaiah 6:10
[5]	Psalm 51:10	[4]	James 3:14
[3]	Romans 6:17	[5]	Jeremiah 17:9
[1]	Psalm 102:4	[4]	1 Samuel 25:37

2. See the relevant scripture(s)

3. See the relevant scripture(s)

4.
- *Romans 2:15* – God has written His Law on men's hearts
- *Matthew 13:19* – God sows His Word into our hearts
- *Ezekiel 11:19* – God will give us a heart that has a desire for Him
- *Romans 10:10* – God puts faith to believe in Him, in our hearts, leading to salvation
- *Romans 5:5* – God has poured His love into our hearts

5. See the relevant scripture(s)

6. a) [6]   b) [4]   c) [2]
   d) [1]   e) [3]   f) [5]

SECTION 6
Still Waiting

Personal Notes

Introduction

The need for right action

In this section we will discover some of the positive effects of waiting on God. Of course, if we want answers from God, we need to ask Him questions, especially about the things which are relevant for that day or our life at that time.

We then need to give God some room so that He can answer. Remember, God answers when the time is right and we must obey God's word to us if we expect Him to speak to us again. God does not waste words on the disobedient. The things which God repeatedly speaks to us are either the really important things or those things which we continue not to obey.

Do not limit your time of waiting on the Lord to just asking questions of Him. Give some time to waiting quietly before Him and allow the Holy Spirit to do as He wills. Time given to God is never time wasted, even when the pressure is on.

> *'Seek the Lord and live.'* (Amos 5:6)

Seeking God demands a total giving of ourselves to God and His purposes (Deuteronomy 4:29; Isaiah 55:6).

> *'You will seek me and find me when you seek me with all your heart.'* (Jeremiah 29:13)

In the sections which follow we will explore some of the outstanding fruit which results from our taking time to wait on the Lord in our daily lives.

Key Verses

Psalm 51:17   John 4:23, 24

Isaiah 40:31   James 4:2, 3

Isaiah 64:4

PART 6.1
Patience

T his is not the kind of patience where we put up with everything and do nothing. It is a dynamic, godly patience.

There are two words for patience in the New Testament. Translated, one means *steadfastness* or *perseverance* and the other means *patience with an image of keeping up the pressure*. God is patient with us in the second way. He keeps leaning on us until we cave in and we let God be God.

> *'Be still before the Lord and wait patiently for him; do not fret when men succeed in their ways, when they carry out their wicked schemes. Refrain from anger and turn from wrath; do not fret, it leads only to evil. For evil men will be cut off, but those who hope in the Lord will inherit the land.'* (Psalm 37:7–9)

When we hear God's word to us, obey it and wait patiently on Him, it is very fruitful and productive in our lives (Luke 8:15).

> *'I wait for the Lord, my soul waits, and in his word I put my hope.'* (Psalm 130:5)

PART 6.2
Rest

'There remains, then, a Sabbath rest for the people of God; for anyone who enters God's rest also rests from his own work.'   (Hebrews 4:9, 10)

Resting in God is drawing aside for a period of time to meet with Him. To rest in God is to know absolute dependence on Him (Psalm 62:1–5). It is to cast all our cares on Him (1 Peter 5:7). It is seeing our lives and circumstances as He does and it is a bringing of our difficulties and placing them at His feet.

When we are tired and our spiritual resources are at a low ebb, the flesh will often demand to be satisfied, e.g. watching TV, eating food, staying up late and not sleeping, sleeping too much etc. It is all right to rest and relax – in fact, it is very important to – but do not give the enemy any victory. Only do things that glorify God.

PART 6.3
Instruction

'Show me your ways, O Lord; teach me your paths. Lead me in your truth and teach me, for you are the God of my salvation; on you I wait all the day.'

                    (Psalm 25:4, 5)

The word of God comes as a consequence of knowing and waiting on God. It gives us the guidance, insight and clarification we need as God's servants (Isaiah 55:8–11). Believers need to know God's strategy on every occasion in order to live victoriously and fruitfully for God (2 Samuel 5:17–25).

Waiting on God allows us to listen to God. It is a poor servant who is deaf to his master's voice! God can use a variety of ways to speak to us including an audible voice, visions, dreams, still small voice, 'hunches', circumstances, other people etc.

Many Christians are good at talking to God, but less good at listening to Him. God often speaks to us in pictorial form because it is easier to remember than words. Also, if what we are hearing is from God, other people will usually be hearing the same thing.

Waiting on God also:

- helps us to discover God's will for our lives.

- helps us to know why God is doing what He is doing.

- enables us to get our spiritual priorities and our time priorities sorted out in God.

- assists us in our decision-making, because we can make decisions out of God's wisdom and revelation rather than human reasoning.

- enables us to get to know what God desires and not just what He requires. Like King David, we will know that the laws of sacrifice were not the total expression of God's will. What God really wanted and still wants is obedience.

PART 6.4
Strength and Refreshment

'They that wait upon the Lord shall renew their strength; they shall mount up with wings as eagles; they shall run, and not be weary; and they shall walk, and not faint.'
(Isaiah 40:31 AV)

'Wait for the Lord; be strong and take heart and wait for the Lord.' (Psalm 27:14)

'For the eyes of the Lord range throughout the earth to strengthen those whose hearts are fully committed to him.' (2 Chronicles 16:9)

Personal Notes

Waiting on God increases our motivation to serve Him. The motivation to serve the Lord, when we genuinely meet with Him and hear His words addressed to us, is great. It seems that there is nothing we would not do for Him and anything seems possible.

Waiting on God also:

- helps restore our motivation to serve Him, because we are sufficiently sorted out in God.

- helps us to receive the rest and reassurance we need in God.

- enables us to regain our confidence and strength, not in ourselves, but in God and His ability to use even us to carry out His will and to live victoriously.

- recharges or refuels our spiritual reserves.

- enables us to continue to face the challenges that are before us in our service for the Lord.

- helps us to overcome discouragement when things go wrong, even when our ministry is removed from us, because our hope is in the Lord and not in what we do for Him.

- assists us to regain our courage, our hope and our desire in the Lord to battle for Him.

PART 6.5
Brokenness

'The sacrifices of God are a broken spirit; a broken and contrite heart, O God, you will not despise.'
(Psalm 51:17)

'The Lord is close to the broken-hearted and saves those who are crushed in spirit.' (Psalm 34:18)

'God has chosen the things that are nothing to bring to nothing the things that are.' (1 Corinthians 1:25–31)

The brokenness we are talking about here, does not come through being crushed. There is a more profound brokenness than any that comes on a horizontal or human level. There is the brokenness of a person who has met the reality of God.

Some of us are broken by circumstances or relationships etc. God can use these things, but eventually they need healing. Those who have been broken by meeting with the reality of God do not need healing (Genesis 32:24–32). If this brokenness was healed, they would be back in the flesh.

PART 6.6
God

'The Spirit is the real living presence and the power of the Father working in us.' (Andrew Murray)

'Since ancient times no-one has heard, no ear has perceived, no eye has seen any God besides you, who acts on behalf of those who wait for him.' (Isaiah 64:4)

God becomes bigger to us and His reign becomes more firmly established in our lives as we wait on Him. The more we express our love for Him, the more we will find we love Him and have love in our life; the more we worship Him, the more we will want to worship Him; the more we thank Him for all His faithfulness and provision, the more grateful we will be for the way He is working in every detail of our life.

What is important in your life? We may want to rush ahead and do great things, but at the end of it all, what will we have achieved? The thing that is really important is to let God be God.

Waiting on God also:

- helps us to develop an attitude of submission to God.

- enables us to reconcile ourselves to God (1 John 1:7–9).

- gets our heart tuned in to God's heart enabling us to feel as He feels.

- helps us to recognise afresh God's love for us (Lamentations 3:22, 23), His willingness to help us (Joshua 1:5; Isaiah 41:10), and His desire to protect, nurture and care for us, His children (Deuteronomy 32:10–13; Psalms 57:1; 91:4; Matthew 23:37).

- enables us to spend quality time with God.

- enlarges our knowledge of God, helping us to see that nothing is impossible for Him and for us, if He so wills it.

- helps us to understand, at least to some extent, the power of God which is far greater than anything in the world and, therefore, get a true, godly perspective of our life and our circumstances.

- enables us to experience the majesty and glory of God.

- builds our relationship with God.

- assists us to worship God for who He is and give Him praise and thanksgiving for all He has done for us.

PART 6.7
Changed Lives

By waiting on the Lord we can transform our self-centredness into God-centredness, because we can more readily see things as God sees them.

When we have met with God and heard His words to us, we need to allow those words to have an effect in us. We do this by obeying them, and allowing them to become part of our lives; by giving them room and meditating on them.

Meditating is like tuning our souls into God and His will, and giving Him the opportunity to work in the areas which He has revealed to us as we have waited on Him. Meditation helps us to personalise and internalise God's words to us so that they become living, active and effective in our lives.

Remember though that the Holy Spirit should be in charge of any time of meditation. Many Christians hear God's word to them, but never obey it or allow it to have the life-changing effect God intended.

PART 6.8
Other Fruits

Waiting on God allows us to:

- give room for the Holy Spirit to search us and work within our lives as God knows He needs to.

- bring God and our point of need together.

- be filled with the Holy Spirit afresh (Ephesians 5:18) and so be filled with the power and strength of God.

- assess where we are at with God with His help.

- understand the reality, significance and true size of our problems and situation in God, i.e. see things from God's perspective.

- gain a growing love for God and for other people.

- receive insight and wisdom from God.

- remember and praise God for His past goodness and faithfulness.

- generate faith that can move mountains.

- have God's peace reigning in our hearts, because it encourages dependence on Him.

- have a child-like trust in God even in the darkest of situations, both inside and outside God's Church.

- gain the power we need in ministry, because we will humbly acknowledge our own lack of power and ask Him to work through us by the power of the Holy Spirit.

PART 6.9
Worship Arises Out of Relationship with God

'To train our people in their worship to wait on God and to make the cultivation of a deeper sense of His presence, of more direct contact with Him, of entire dependence on Him, is a definite aim in our ministry.'

(Andrew Murray)

Worship should not just be an activity or experience carried out during Christian meetings, it should be the lifestyle of every believer.

Everything we do as Christians should be an act of worship of God. Of course, this does not mean we go around singing songs 24 hours a day. Worship is offering or giving ourselves to God; being totally available and totally obedient to Him.

It arises out of our relationship with God and so its depth should increase as our relationship with God matures. God wants this response from us and so we should be seeking to develop an ever deepening relationship with Him. God does not demand this of us. He wants us to choose to do this. Our heavenly Father is seeking people who will worship Him in spirit and in truth (John 4:23, 24) – let's not disappoint Him! True praise and worship also gives us a God-awareness that takes away our self-awareness and so it is an important part of waiting on the Lord.

PART 6.10
Knowing the Reasons for Failed Times of Waiting on the Lord

There are many reasons why it seems as though our waiting on God has not been fruitful. Among these we might consider the following:

- We are so dry spiritually and God seems so far away that we do not recognise the need for input from God in order to be able to get right with Him and to be able to minister to others.

- Tiredness or fatigue prevents us from concentrating.

- Personal burdens which cause us to be so preoccupied with our own problems that we do not go to God.

- Just using our quiet times as study periods. We, therefore, do not meet with God, do not listen to Him, and do not make room in our lives to enable God's specific word to us to have an effect, i.e. there is no life in it.

- Thinking that we do not have the time or rushing our times of waiting on the Lord.

- We are so bored with our quiet time that our heart is not in it.

- Indiscipline.

- Discouragement, i.e. we are failing and it turns us from God, instead of to Him.

- Wrong priorities.

- Too much noise or too many distractions.

- Failure to obey God when He speaks to us. We should have a deep desire within us to obey whatever God tells us to do during our times of waiting on Him. Many Christians fail to hear from God, because they stubbornly refuse to obey His directives to them.

Action Study: *Learning to Wait on God*

Take the following simple outline as a starting point in your experience of waiting on God. This introduces five aspects of this spiritual exercise.

- *Learning to know His presence*
- *Learning to hear His word*
- *Learning to pray in the spirit*
- *Learning to cast your care on Him*
- *Learning to wait on God for others*

1. *Learning to know His presence*

   Look up and complete the following scriptures:

   - Psalm 46:10:

     '*Be* _____ *and* _____ *that* _____ .'

   - Jeremiah 29:13:

     '*You will* _____ *and find me* _____ *with all your heart. I will* _____ .'

   - Hebrews 4:9, 10:

     '*There remains, then,* _____ *for the people of God; for anyone* _____ *also rests* _____ .'

Four simple steps

- **Lay aside distractions**
  We are surrounded by technology, hustle and bustle and busyness on every side. It can be strange for us modern people to try and be still in mind and spirit for more than a few seconds.

  Sit quietly and ask the Lord for inner peace and quiet. Practise leaving everything else aside.

- **Activate your spirit**
  You can do this by quietly singing a spiritual song or by listening to and then joining in with some spiritual music. Or you can do it by focusing on a spiritual thought or by quietly praying in tongues.

- **Focus in on God**
  Do not focus on your own agenda of personal need, nor on an agenda of intercession for others – not yet. Instead focus on some fact(s) about God. Take the words of David from Psalm 103: *'Bless the Lord, O my soul, and all that is within me, bless His holy name.'*

  Take a simple scripture which speaks about God in some way and let that be the focus of your spiritual attention. Magnify (that is give Him more space, make Him bigger in your heart and mind) by praising Him.

- **Ask the Lord to make Himself known to you in the Spirit**
  The promise of the Scriptures is that God will make Himself known to those who seek Him.

2. *Learning to hear His word*

Complete the following scripture from Psalm 130:5:

> *'I* _____ , *my soul*
>
> *waits, and* _____ .'

At first we need to meditate on what we know to be God's Word, namely, the Scriptures. The discipline of meditating on Scripture cultivates a sensitive spirit in us to the voice of God and develops a maturity in understanding of His truth and ways.

To start anywhere else is to be in danger of rank subjectivism. Our spirit is sensitised by the revelation of Scripture and is thus prepared for hearing from God through other means such as direct words, dreams or visions.

Six simple steps

- **Obtain a suitable version of the Scriptures**
  This means one that you easily understand but not a paraphrase, e.g. the New International Version or the New King James.

- **Ask God**
  The Scriptures tell us to do just this (see James 1:5).

- **Confess your desire to walk in God's ways**
  (see Psalm 1:1)

- **Focus on a particular word, verse or passage**
  (see Jeremiah 15:16)

- **Write down what you hear or understand**

- **Put into practice anything God tells you to do**
  (see James 1:27)

3. *Learning to pray in the spirit*

   Paul speaks about this in 1 Corinthians 14:13–17. In talking about a person 'praying with his spirit' he is alluding to something which is more private than public – that is, speaking to God in tongues on our own. In fact, he says that we should not engage in this publicly without an interpretation of what we say for everyone's benefit (1 Corinthians 14:27–28).

   Check the following scriptures:

   - Jude 20:

     'But you, dear friends, build yourselves up in _____

     _____ and _____

     _____ .'

- Ephesians 6:18:

  'Pray _____

  _____ *.'*

Praying in the spirit, that is, using a private gift of tongues, leads to personal edification (1 Corinthians 14:4) and is essential in the sphere of spiritual warfare (Ephesians 6:18).

If you have never prayed in tongues, which is a God-given language, do not strive or worry. Ask God to release this gift in you by the Holy Spirit. Do not be afraid or hesitant to speak out what the Holy Spirit puts on your tongue. Through time you will come to recognise the different ways by which the Holy Spirit operates through you in this area and your confidence will increase with practise.

4. ***Learning to cast your care on Him***

Complete the following scripture from 1 Peter 5:7:

  'Cast all _____ *on him*

  because he _____ *.'*

This is one exercise which is indispensable if we are to be effective in our life for God. Life is filled with so many distractions and burdens that unless we learn to transfer the load to the Lord we risk being swamped by them.

Four simple steps

- **Share your burden honestly with God** – if necessary, write it down so that you express it.

- **Take the words of 1 Peter 5:7** (above) and speak them to yourself asking the Lord to give you a sense of 'unloading' in your spirit.

- **In your spirit actively transfer the burden from yourself to God** – load it on to Him. If it helps, physically enact the transaction with your hands.

- **Claim the strength and help of the Holy Spirit** – to enable you to live continually from now with a sense of relief from this burden.

5. ***Learning to wait on God for others***

In normal terms we call this intercession. However, as we wait on God our prayers of intercession can be based on direct revelation rather than the normal prayer list. It is an invigorating experience to know the leading of the Holy Spirit in this way. He can lead our spirits directly showing us for whom to pray and exactly how to pray for them.

The result is that we have a sense of being directly involved in God's current agenda and a sense of privilege at being permitted to share in His divine action at this particular moment.

Fill in the blanks in Isaiah 64:4:

'Since ancient times no one has heard, _____

_____ , no eye has seen

any God besides you, who _____

_____ .'

Four simple steps

- **Follow** the promptings of the Spirit.

- **Make a note** of particular features of the prompting.

- **Pray** into and about this revelation.

- **Wait and watch** for an answer or response to exercise of your spirit.

Answers

This is a personal exercise so there are no answers. See the relevant scriptures to check that you have filled the blanks in correctly.

SECTION 7
Growing in God

Introduction

The need for growth

'But grow in the grace and knowledge of our Lord and Saviour Jesus Christ. To him be glory both now and for ever! Amen.'   (2 Peter 3:18)

Just as we expect a child to grow in the natural, so God expects His spiritual children to grow in knowledge of Him, in maturity, in effectiveness and in love.

Every Christian is designed by God to grow in Christ. In fact, as Christians we should be progressively becoming more Christ-like day by day. This will not happen if we sit about and do nothing; it will only occur if we make ourselves available to God. He wants us to become usable, prepared vessels who are ready for His use.

God has a plan for each one of our lives, but we have a part to play in its fulfilment. We need to yield our lives over to God and let Him work out that plan. In the meantime, we should be getting on with what He has already shown us to do.

Key Verses

Romans 12:3–8   2 Peter 3:18

Ephesians 2:10   1 John 3:11–24

2 Peter 1:5–8

PART 7.1
Crisis or Continuous Growth

There are two different ways or processes in which we grow spiritually. The first, *crisis growth*, describes the place of urgent events and circumstances which overtake us and cause growth through response to challenge. The second, *continuous growth*, is a steady pattern of growth which results from our learning the ongoing lessons of life and our continual response to the teachings of Scripture. The diagram below illustrates these two ways of growth.

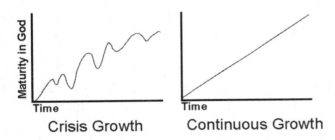

i) Crisis growth

This is when the Holy Spirit moves in us powerfully to bring about a tremendous and immediate challenge to our life. Here, there is a crisis that develops in our spirit and we have to do something about it.

God, through the ministry of the Holy Spirit, will use these experiences to challenge some blockage or some defence that has prevented or hindered our spiritual growth. As we yield these areas to God, He begins to deal with them.

ii) Continuous growth

This is slow, but steady, growth towards maturity, which is brought about by continual openness and obedience to God. It is being able realistically to appraise our life on a daily basis and see that our growth is steadily going up, instead of up and down.

iii) **What to watch out for**

We must not become crisis-related people. This kind of person is only able to enter into the things of God when things are emotionally charged, red-hot or hyped-up. Crises tend to be very emotional experiences and, therefore, the many Christians who run on crisis growth have an extremely emotional faith. Their lives go up and down spiritually and they become 'crisis addicts'. They need a crisis to make them feel stimulated and to keep them going.

If we begin to understand the principles of discipleship, obedience to the Word of God, and relationship with God, we will also understand that the basis for our growth in Christ does not depend on our feelings (whether good, bad or ugly), but rather it depends on the factors we build into our lives as we follow after God.

This does not mean to say that we will not need or have crisis growth experiences with God. It just means that the crisis times need to be contained within our continuous growth.

PART 7.2
Effectiveness for God

i) **Keeping our balance**

God wants us to live with a continual openness to Him and His Word, instead of leap-frogging from one crisis to another. Some people are not happy if they are not weeping all the time. These people tend to be very unstable, because they find it difficult to make the clear-headed, clear-minded and clear-hearted decisions that all Christians need to make.

We will never enter into a powerful ministry, have victory in spiritual warfare, or be useful to God, if we live out of a crisis base all the time. This is because we will be so vulnerable to our emotions that we will never be able to get outside ourselves and take a grip of the situation.

Growth is not just about being sorted out (although it includes this), it is about getting to grips with the factors which actually lead us to a place of openness and obedience to God. Our lives should be continually progressing towards maturity in God and we should be progressively becoming more effective for God.

People who mainly rely on crisis times for their growth tend to be rather selfish in their Christian lives. As Christians, we need to be people who see things from God's perspective. When we do this, the mountain-size problems will become molehill-size ones. We will be looking for what we can do for God, instead of what He can do for us.

If we can get God's perspective on a situation, we will be able to help other people through their crisis times. We will only be able to deal with such crises, if we have begun to live in a continuum of openness to the Lord ourselves. If we are living from one crisis to another of repentance, weeping or even revival, and our emotions are continually open and vulnerable, and our nerves, spiritually speaking, are on the edge, we will not be able objectively and clear-headedly, to handle the big issues that relate to other people or that relate to some other thing that needs to be done in the Kingdom of God.

ii) **The best way**

The best way to grow in God is to develop the more stable foundation of continuous growth, while at the same time staying open to God so that He always has the opportunity to break in and introduce a crisis time with Him if needs be.

We need crisis times with God in order to get cleaned out or overcome a certain problem in our life. Crisis times are usually the way God chooses to move us onto a higher plane with Him, because they break down the barriers that have prevented us from moving on this level in God. Crisis and continuous growth are both valid and necessary parts of Christian growth.

PART 7.3
A Practical Illustration

A helicopter can do most things its pilot wants it to do. The secret of flying one is to learn how to bring the machine into balance and so keep it on the level. Before starting to fly, the pilot learns to do this by holding onto a piece of glass by an attached handle, and trying to keep a ball-bearing exactly in the middle of the glass by counter-balancing as the ball-bearing moves about. By doing this, the would-be pilot develops an amazing sense of fine tuning and an incredible sense of objectivity to the ball-bearing.

This illustration can teach us some good lessons. If we want to see spiritual growth in our lives, we need to be able to see where we are in relation to everything around us. Through the Holy Spirit, we should be able to perceive what fine tuning is needed to keep our life at its right angle, in order to keep everything stable and level. It is only then that we will stay effective and fruitful for God, no matter what situation we are in.

So many Christians react to the situations that confront them in the wrong way and it causes them to become unstable, non-functional and even dangerous. Christians need, with the help of the Holy Spirit, the ability to observe themselves in the middle of all the shifts of life.

They will then know how to re-adjust themselves, so that they can stay in a place of effectiveness for God, no matter where they are or what they are going through. We can sing choruses and be on our knees in repentance all day long, seven days a week, and still not know how to re-adjust our lives in order to keep them in balance.

We must ask God for spiritual wisdom, discernment and instruction and we must ask the right questions of ourselves. If we want to function effectively in ministry, we need to get more than the anointing of healing or the gift of being able to preach, and so on, we need to be able to stand back inside ourselves and watch the play of events happening in front of us, and, in the Spirit, take control.

Maturity in God is keeping our lives on a level plane, even when turbulence or trouble comes. Immature people sink or get knocked off course during such times. We need to be able to stay level in any situation and so cope with trouble, overcoming it by adjusting our lives in the appropriate way. To do this, we need to understand ourselves and know how we react to certain situations. Beyond this, we need to know what to do in the situation in order to take control and to give room for God to be able to use us in the situation. This is how to live in victory and how to stay useful to God in whatever situation He puts us.

PART 7.4
Areas in Which We Need to Grow

When we speak about growing up we obviously have in mind more than just the physical aspects of development. There are other elements of growth which are utterly important and which need to go along with physical growth. In spiritual terms, these are the areas of *character*, *capacity*, *understanding* and *relationships*. Each area has a question that every Christian needs to ask themselves, if they want to be fruitful for God.

i) Character

This is the development of personality, identity, integrity, and morality. ***The question to ask yourself here is***:

Who am I?

When we become a Christian, we do not immediately lose our old character and personality. The truth is that we are far from perfect when we first come to know God and our knowledge of Him is very limited. What we need to do is give our lives to Him so that He can begin to teach us and mould us into what He needs us to be. Part of this teaching process is discovering who we are in Christ, and part of it is knowing who we are in ourselves.

Personal Notes

We should never use the phrase, 'who we are in Christ', as a cover-up for actually facing the truth about ourselves. We need to know our strengths and weaknesses, and we need to know if we have any character flaws or spiritual bondages. It is never right to ignore these things or to say that they are not there, when in reality they are things that are huge issues in our lives.

Knowing who we are is a very liberating discovery. We will then see why we react as we do when confronted with certain situations; we will know when we are out of our depth or moving into a danger area, and we will know our strengths and where we can be of help to others.

We need to know who we are, so that we can be real with ourselves. It is because we do not know who we are that we come under bondage to all sorts of things, e.g. yielding to the pressure from other people who want us to do something that we know we are not equipped to do. When we know who we are, we can live as God intends us to, doing the work He has prepared in advance for us to do.

This all may sound very simple, but I think today we have got so complex that we get frightened by simplicity. God wants to take us on into maturity in Him and He does not want to make it so complicated that no one can attain it. God wants things to be straightforward; He wants His directions to us to be so clear that even the most stupid of us cannot miss the way.

> '*A main road will go through that once-deserted land; it will be named "The Holy Highway". No evil-hearted men may walk upon it. God will walk there with you; even the most stupid cannot miss the way.*' (Isaiah 35:8 Living Bible)

ii) Capability

This is the development of gift and talent. ***The question to ask yourself here is***:

What can I do?

In the world at large, this is a question we are confronted with and have to answer, time and time again. Your answer to this question will usually determine the job that you do.

As Christians, we need to answer this question in spiritual terms. We are not rendered helpless the moment we are filled with the Holy Spirit, but rather we need to ask ourselves bluntly, with the help of the Holy Spirit's insight, 'What can I do?'

A lot of us live in unreality here, because we want to do something that someone else is doing. The truth is that we can never copy another person in spiritual terms. God has gifted us all differently. Instead of living with a false, hyped-up ideal of what we can do for God, we need to ask the question, 'What can I do?', and then actually live in the call that God has placed on our lives.

It must be remembered that our capacity in God is only limited by our faith and by what we have been called by Him to do. We can do anything, if it is necessary for the fulfilment of God's will (Philippians 4:13, 19). God does not, however, take our lives over. He uses what is there and what we make available to Him. It is the power of God working through who we are and what we know that allows us to achieve anything for God.

iii) Understanding

This is the development of intellectual capacity, insight, sensitivity, and perception. *The question to ask yourself here is*:

What do I know?

It is amazing that we submit ourselves to examinations, to tests and to discussions which explore our understanding of given subjects, but when it comes to spiritual things, many of us run away and avoid the issue of 'What do I know?'

As Christians, we need to develop our knowledge of the things and ways of God, particularly in the areas to which we are called. We need to give our lives to God, disciplining them so that we grow intellectually, and so that our discernment and insight matures. These are the things that will enable us to be more fruitful and effective for God.

iv) Relationships

This is the capacity to integrate with other human beings on formal and personal levels. *The question to ask yourself here is*:

How do I relate?

How do you get on with people in the variety of circumstances in which you meet them? We need to grow in this area, especially if we want to be able to serve other people. All Christians are called by God to interrelate and to love each other (1 John 3:11–24).

We need to be developing in this important area, if we are going to be effective for God. Jesus showed us God's ideal. He was a man who grew in favour with other men as He grew up (Luke 2:52). He earned the right to speak into many people's lives, because of the relationship and rapport He developed with them.

Effective ministry usually arises out of relationship, and submission certainly does. The need to develop in the area of relationships does not mean that we have to have everybody as our best friends, but it does mean that we need to learn how to relate to others.

Notice how these questions relate to each other. Who you are will determine what you can do, what you can know and to whom you relate. Some people are able to retain knowledge and get it organised in such a way that they can teach it to others. Other people have a developed intuitive sense and so seem to be able to discern things about people. Knowing that God wants you to be a preacher, for example, lays a demand upon your life to assimilate more spiritual and Bible knowledge. If you find it very difficult to relate to people, it is highly unlikely that God will call you to be a pastor.

These four questions are fundamental and we need to address ourselves to them if we are going to know spiritual growth.

Bible Study: *Amazing Grace*

G race is one of the most powerful yet least understood themes of the New Testament. We tend to operate with an inert view of grace which is summed up in the traditional definition that grace is 'God's unmerited favour'. There is no doubt that this is true because in Christ we have received all that we did not deserve.

However, when we examine the New Testament more closely we will see that grace is an active force which releases the power of God into our lives and is the means by which we can fulfil the will of God for our lives. This view of grace is more clearly expressed in the words of James Ryle:

'**Grace** is the empowering presence of God enabling me to be what God has created me to be and to do what God has called me to do.'

1. *Effective grace*

   Check the following New Testament scriptures in the light of this definition and observe for yourself the real power of grace at work.

John 1:14, 16	1 Timothy 1:14
Acts 4:33; 6:8; 18:27	Hebrews 4:16
Romans 5:20, 21	James 4:6
2 Corinthians 12:9	2 Peter 3:18
Galatians 1:3	

2. *An active force*

   Complete the following scriptures as see how real grace is in its action for us.

   - Titus 2:11:

     'For the grace of God _____

     _____ has appeared.'

- Acts 15:11:

  'We believe it _____ of our

  Lord Jesus Christ, _____ ,

  just as they are.'

- Romans 5:15:

  'How much more _____ and the

  _____ of the one

  man, Jesus Christ, _____ to many.'

Match the right scriptures with the appropriate characteristic of grace:

a) ☐ 2 Peter 1:2, 3   1) personal

b) ☐ Ephesians 1:7   2) living

c) ☐ 2 Peter 3:18   3) active

d) ☐ 2 Corinthians 12:9   4) enabling

e) ☐ Ephesians 3:7   5) dynamic

3. *Saving grace*

Salvation is not something that is static in the experience of the believer. Rather it is an ongoing process in which the Holy Spirit is continually releasing the active power of grace into our lives and by which He is changing us more and more into the likeness of Christ.

What three dimensions of salvation do the following scriptures reveal?

Ephesians 2:8 _____

1 Corinthians 1:18 _____

Romans 5:9 _____

Complete the following scripture (Titus 2:11–12) which brings all these three together:

'For the _____ that _____

_____ has appeared to all men.

_____ to say "No"

_____ and worldly passions

and to _____

_____ in this present age

while we wait _____

_____ .'

4.   *The abundance of grace*

Romans chapter 5 is one of the greatest 'grace' passages in the New Testament. It teaches us some of the most important lessons about grace and shows us its tremendous breadth and length.

a)   **The effective presence of grace** (Romans 5:1, 2)

'We have _____ through our

Lord Jesus Christ, through whom _____

_____ into this grace

in which _____ .'

b)   **The manifold purpose of grace** (Romans 5:15)

'For if the many _____ of the

one man, how much more _____

and the gift that came by the grace _____

_____ .'

c) **The abundant provision of grace** (Romans 5:17)

'How much more will those who _____

_____ and of the gift of

righteousness _____ through

the one man, Jesus Christ.'

d) **The overwhelming power of grace** (Romans 5:20)

'Where _____ , grace

_____ .'

e) **The ultimate perspective of grace** (Romans 5:21)

'Just as _____ , so also

grace _____

to bring eternal life through Jesus Christ our Lord.'

It is no wonder then that Paul goes on to make the practical appeal in Romans 6:12–14 to all who have come to know the power of this grace in their lives. Complete the blanks:

'Therefore do not _____ in your

mortal body so that _____ .

Do not _____ of your body to sin,

as _____ , but rather

offer yourselves to God, as those who have been

brought _____ ; and offer the

parts of your body to him _____

_____ . For sin shall not

_____ , because you are

not under law, but _____ .'

Answers

1. Personal

2. See the relevant scripture(s)

    a) ⬚3   b) ⬚1   c) ⬚2
    d) ⬚5   e) ⬚4

3. *Ephesians 2:8*:   **Have been** saved

    1 Corinthians 1:18:   **Are being** saved

    Romans 5:9:   **Will be** saved

4. See the relevant scripture(s)

SECTION 8
Growth Factors

Introduction

Means to an end

S piritual growth is such an important subject for the believer that we will continue to look at other aspects of it in this section.

The process of our development and growth as a Christian is aided by what we can call certain important *growth factors*. These factors are means which operate in all our lives and cause us to grow if we react to them properly. This is as true in our spiritual life as it is in the natural. In this section we will look at *six important growth factors* as they relate to the development and deepening of our Christian lives.

Key Verses

Proverbs 22:6

Romans 12:2

1 Corinthians 4:15, 16

Philippians 4:11–13

Hebrews 5:11–14

1 John 3:16–18

PART 8.1
Instruction

'Train a child in the way he should go, and when he is old he will not turn from it.'   (Proverbs 22:6)

Many Christians have not developed their minds for God to any real extent. This does not call for intellectual prowess, but for submission to the discipline of studying the Word of God and growing in our understanding and grasp of the things of God.

Some course of study/application/training is good for every one of us. Christians, who are not fed or being nourished on the Word of God and who do not know how to divide the word of truth correctly, are ignoring at their peril the main enabler of their spiritual growth. All Christians need to apply themselves to the Word of God in order to get to know God and be instructed in His ways (Hebrews 5:11–14; 2 Timothy 3:14–17).

'Do your best to present yourselves to God as one approved, a workman who does not need to be ashamed and who correctly handles the word of truth.'
(2 Timothy 2:15)

Too many Christians have untidy minds. Some of our minds are like the forgotten attic at the top of a four-storey house – we know it's there, but we do not know quite what's in it! We need to do a stocktake of what is in our minds. This will stop us living in unreality as far as our minds are concerned.

We need our minds to be renewed. This is an active, very practical, feet-on-the-ground thing. We do not get our mind renewed by just sitting and thinking nice thoughts – we get a renewed mind by discipline and by allowing the Holy Spirit to be Lord of it (Luke 8:15; Romans 12:2; Ephesians 4:22–24).

The Bible tells us that we have the mind of Christ (1 Corinthians 2:10–16). If this is the case, we have the mind of God at our disposal and, therefore, we should be some of the most creative, intelligent people on earth. We are people who have access to the mind of the living God. The trouble is that many Christians have put their minds in neutral, instead of sharpening them as useful tools for God which He can use as He sees fit. Study is probably the best way of preparing our minds, and what better book to study than the Word of God?

If we aspire to being used by God then we cannot afford to be lazy. God is looking for quality people to place into servanthood in His Body, the Church. God-anointed servants can never stop growing in God; they should never live off their past reputation or past revelation; they need to be constantly coming to God and His Word and so keeping their minds sharp, active and useful to Him.

As Christians, we should be exciting each other with the Word of God, because there is a wealth of treasure stored therein. God wants us to be continually fed with His living Word and never to lapse into spiritual lethargy. We need to stimulate our minds before God by studying His Word, and we need to be able to think clearly and creatively for God. God is not going to do for us what we need to be doing for ourselves. He has provided the material to study and He has given us the mind with which to study; now it's up to us!

As time goes by, we ought to be able to grasp more of the truth of God and understand more about God. Then, we will no longer be people who are blown here and there by every wind of teaching that comes our way (Ephesians 4:14). The Church of God needs people like this far more today than it ever did.

Instruction bears fruit through:

- the development of a disciplined mind.

- heightening our ability to concentrate.

- creating a growing awareness of our abilities and gifts.

- bringing a discipline to the use of our time.

- developing the basic disciplines of communication, i.e. reading, expression and research.

- growth in personal confidence as we progress.

- teaching us how to handle the things we dislike or find difficult.

PART 8.2
Inspiration

'Even though you have ten thousand guardians in Christ, you do not have many fathers, for in Christ Jesus I became your father through the gospel. Therefore I urge you to imitate me.'   (1 Corinthians 4:15, 16)

There is an amazing stimulation to spiritual growth when we can find, with the help of God, a person who is setting an example of living in Christ that is worth imitating. Of course, we should never attempt to become a carbon-copy of such a person or a competitor, but we can be inspired and stimulated by them. These people encourage us to say, 'Oh God, let me be like that,' or even, 'If they can do it, so can I!' (2 Timothy 1:5; 3:10; Titus 2:7, 8; Hebrews 13:7).

The apostle Paul was such an inspiration to the Corinthian church, not just because he brought them to spiritual birth or because he gave them their doctrine, but because he stood in their life as the tremendous 'spark-plug' of the Holy Spirit. He put in what was necessary at the right time in order to bring about a dynamic movement of the Holy Spirit in their lives. Not many of us could say like Paul, 'Imitate me!'

The Church today needs more people who are an inspiration to others. These people are 'spark' people, who do not just have flat knowledge, legalistic commitment or bland perseverance, but have something else; a plus factor that makes all the difference. These people are inspired and they, in turn, become an inspiration to others. They have a flame in their hearts that lights something in our hearts. Inspiration is a tremendous stimulus to spiritual growth.

There is no one person who is complete or total as far as inspiration is concerned (with the exception of Jesus Christ). Therefore, be careful never to take your inspiration from just one person, because this tends to lead to hero worship. God will show you the people from whom you should gain your inspiration, if you stay open to Him. If you do this, those you gain inspiration from will enlarge your heart, vision and ministry.

Such people do not necessarily have to be alive; you may gain your inspiration by what they have written, said or done, or what has been written about them. They also do not necessarily have to be Christians.

We need to find people who inspire us, so that our own growth in God is stimulated. *It may be that different people will inspire us in different areas.* For example:

- in the development of life and character

- in the area of achievement and application

- in relation to the exercise of a particular gifting

- in the question of commitment and perseverance

- in bearing the responsibility of leadership

PART 8.3
Adversity

'Give thanks in all circumstances, for this is God's will for you in Christ Jesus.'   (1 Thessalonians 5:18)

Notice that this verse does not say, 'thank God for all circumstances', but rather 'thank God in all circumstances'. There is quite a powerful difference between these two statements, even though just one word has been changed.

If you are thanking God *for* all circumstances, you will be thanking Him for all the things He did not mean to be laid on you. If, however, you thank God *in* all circumstances, then you will be learning from your circumstances and keeping the right attitude within them. You will know that God is in control and you will let your circumstances become your teacher in those moments.

Obviously, you need to stay tuned-in to God in order to know what He wants you to do in the situation, but you must never think that satan is in control. If you are a Christian, Jesus is your Lord. He may let you be tempted by the enemy at times, but He has also promised never to let you be tempted beyond what you can bear. He has even promised to give you a way out from the temptation so that you can stand up under it (1 Corinthians 10:13).

> *'That is why, for Christ's sake, I delight in weakness, in insults, in hardships, in persecutions, in difficulties. For when I am weak, then I am strong.'*
> (2 Corinthians 12:10)

The Scriptures make it clear that, whilst we live in the victory of Christ daily, this does not mean that we avoid thereby the warp and woof of human experience. As Amy Carmichael once pointed out, 'It is not the circumstances that are of greatest importance, but our reactions to them.'

Under adversity, we discover some of the greatest realities of our spiritual experience, apart from which we cannot be said to have grown at all in terms of maturity in God (2 Corinthians 4:7–18; Philippians 4:11–13; 2 Timothy 2:3; Hebrews 12:7–11; James 1:2–4).

The test of adversity:

- **exposes the bedrock of our experience**. It takes trouble or difficulty to show us on which rock we stand. If we have built any part of our lives on sandy foundations, it would be better if it collapsed and we could start again on proper foundations.

- **highlights the true values of life**. Life gets out of perspective when everything is dead easy. It gets 'cushy' and we get 'cushy' with it. Many of us think that when the slightest triviality goes wrong, it is a world of importance. However, when we get into real trouble or adversity, we soon realise that all the trivial things are totally unimportant. Adversity brings us back to reality, because it contrasts what is really important with what is not.

Personal Notes

- **brings pressure which demonstrates our character weaknesses and strengths**. Every diamond has flaws, and the secret of making the most of that diamond is not to ignore the flaws, but rather to use them. Diamond cutters scrutinise the diamond, discover the location of the flaws and cut the diamond accordingly. If they did not scrutinise it first and take into account what was there, they would never be able to bring out the diamond's full potential beauty.

- **develops our ability to persevere in faith** through all circumstances. According to the Bible, trials and suffering for the sake of Christ are a normal part of everyday life as a Christian. Of course, we should never let the enemy have any form of victory over us by sitting under something that God never intended for us. We need to seek God and see what He would have us do in every situation, resisting the enemy, if needs be. Remember though, not all problems find their source in the work of the devil.

Life, for many Christians, has only got two symbols; one plus, which equals God; and one minus, which equals the devil. So when something goes right, they say it is God; and when something goes wrong, they say it is the devil. This is not the truth. Some things that appear negative come from God, e.g. when He disciplines us (God only disciplines us for our good, but no discipline seems pleasant at the time, Hebrews 12:5–11).

God wants us to take on the right problems and overcome them in His strength. He wants us to be willing to do whatever He asks, despite the cost to ourselves. We should never fear the circumstances in which we find ourselves, because we should know that God is in control, both of our lives and our circumstances.

- **builds into our lives sensitivity and empathy** to the needs of others, e.g. a person who has suffered is able to empathise with a suffering person.

PART 8.4
Experience

'I know what it is to be in need, and I know what it is to have plenty. I have learned the secret of being content in any and every situation, whether well fed or hungry, whether living in plenty or in want. I can do everything through him who gives me strength.'

(Philippians 4:12, 13)

We need to learn the secret of being content whatever our circumstances, because then we will always be in a position to be fruitful for God, no matter what we are going through. This does not mean that we should lie back and have a totally passive attitude to every situation, but rather it means that we should put our confidence in God and trust Him.

Our diaries should be a record of our spiritual growth. We can either learn from and grow within our circumstances, or we can be damaged by them.

Our experience can be creative or it can be 'water under the bridge' that has little affect upon our lives. There is no substitute for a 'hands-on' experience of life. Experience is a great teacher, if we are open to the lessons it can teach us. Very little beats experience.

Experience is a great teacher, if we learn its lessons properly:

- **It provides a test bed for our ideas, doctrine, and vision**. Your doctrine, your ideas, your vision, or your word from the Lord has got to work out in experience or it is false (Deuteronomy 18:21, 22).

- **It knocks the rough edges off our character** and provides the melting pot of change for our personalities. Experience, whether good or bad, changes us.

- **It develops practical wisdom in us**, so that we are able to learn how to handle a diversity of challenges; for example: disagreement, crisis, challenges to our confidence, new ideas, and different situations in which we have never been before.

- **It promotes self-awareness** – the way we react to experience shows who we really are inside.

PART 8.5
Challenge

'Forgetting what is behind and straining towards what is ahead, I press on towards the goal to win the prize for which God has called me heavenwards in Christ Jesus.'
(Philippians 3:13, 14)

There are two words between which many people do not know the difference. The first word is *react* and the second is the word *respond*.

These words may look the same, but they are in reality totally different. The fact is that most of us spend our time reacting rather than responding. Reaction is what you do when you get a stimulus. It is a 'knee-jerk' reflex, i.e. an immediate action as a direct result of a certain type of stimulus; there is no thought, only action. It is to say 'we have been here before and this is what we did last time.'

Response, however, is different. It is actually taking a minute to allow God, by the Holy Spirit, to gather together all the factors in the situation and to evaluate them in such a way that appropriate action is enabled. Responding is allowing God into the situation. This may only need a split second, but in this small gap amazing things can happen. This is because it allows room for spiritual wisdom and insight, and even innate intuition.

It is important to learn how to respond rather than react, because then we will become more creative and fruitful for God in our lives. We will be more able to handle our experiences and less likely to suffer from them. We will know what will obliterate us and what will be fruitful. Reacting is acting from immediate feeling, whereas responding is letting God in and then doing God's thing in response to a stimulus.

Change is not a passing fad, it is something with which every person needs to come to grips. This does not mean, however, that we should have no stability as Christians. We need something that is stable and will survive no matter what the devil does. God has provided and will provide the stability we need. We need to rest in Him!

To the believer, challenge and change can be a tremendous stimulus to growth because:

- It shows us where our real security lies.

- It provides fresh stimulus and inspiration, and it calls for the setting of fresh goals.

- It provides a breeding ground for faith.

- It prevents boredom and staleness coming into our Christian lives.

- It enlarges our heart by causing us to become more open people.

PART 8.6
Relationships

'We love because he first loved us. If anyone says, "I love God", yet hates his brother, he is a liar. For anyone who does not love his brother, whom he has seen, cannot love God, whom he has not seen.'   (1 John 4:19, 20)

The whole thing about relationships is to know how to integrate with people. As Christians we need to learn how to relate to people. We are Christ's ambassadors on earth and we need to be able to represent Him to those to whom we relate (John 13:35; 1 Corinthians 1:10–17; Philippians 2:1–5; 1 Timothy 5:1, 2; 1 John 3:16–18).

People come in many different forms. The secret of maturity lies in knowing how to respond, rather than react to them. The list below suggests some of the types of people we need to deal with day by day. *Remember, to others, you may be one of these types*:

- stimulating

- aggravating

- frustrating

- enriching

- challenging

- puzzling – and many more

Relationships play some very crucial functions in the area of our own spiritual growth, because they:

- Expose our own inner attitudes.

- Test our reactions to a whole range of different situations and attitudes.

- Bring our own fears and insecurities to the surface, and highlight the threats we feel within ourselves.

- Develop our capacity for personal relationships.

- Provide a context for the growth of a servant heart in relation to others.

- Challenge the possessiveness and selfishness within our own nature.

- Teach us how to handle people.

Assignment

The purpose of this exercise is to help you review what you have just learned in Section 8. Knowledge is, as they say, power. This means that when we understand something clearly such understanding will enable us to put into practice what we know. This is the secret of effective discipleship.

1. The following are some of the important factors which cause us to grow. Match the correct scripture with the appropriate factor.

    a) ☐ 2 Timothy 2:15   1) adversity

    b) ☐ 1 Corinthians 4:15, 16   2) instruction

    c) ☐ 2 Corinthians 12:10   3) relationships

    d) ☐ Philippians 4:12, 13   4) challenge

    e) ☐ Philippians 3:13, 14   5) experience

    f) ☐ John 13:35   6) inspiration

2. Our growth and development is stimulated by a number of significant factors. We might call these *growth factors* since they play such a vital role in our personal development. As we have seen, all these *growth factors* produce fruit in their own distinctive ways. Make a list of the positive effects of the following *growth factors*:

    a) Instruction

    _____

    _____

    _____

    _____

    _____

    _____

b) Experience

_____

_____

_____

_____

c) Challenge

_____

_____

_____

_____

_____

3. Fill in the following scripture (1 Corinthians 4:15, 16) to discover an important principle which the Apostle Paul taught the believers in Corinth.

    'Even though you have _____

    _____ *, you do not*

    _____ *, for in Christ Jesus*

    _____ *through the gospel.*

    Therefore I urge you _____ *.'*

We can all draw great inspiration from the witness of other people's lives and achievements. List the sorts of areas in which we might find such inspiration.

_____

_____

_____

_____

_____

_____

4.   Complete the following scripture (2 Corinthians 4:7–10):

'We have this _____ in jars of clay to

show that this _____

is from God and not from us. We are _____

_____ on every side, but not _____;

perplexed, but _____;

_____ but not abandoned;

_____ but not _____ .

We always carry around in our body _____

_____ , so that the _____

may also be _____ .'

What growth factor is Paul referring to here?

_____

_____

5.   Make a list of the significant benefits adversity brings to our experience.

_____

_____

_____

_____

_____

_____

_____

_____

_____

6. A famous writer once said that 'no man is an island.' We live and work with other people; we need other people to relate to and learn from. What are some of the important effects of relationships with regard to our own maturity?

    _____

    _____

    _____

    _____

    _____

    _____

    _____

    _____

7. In what way has this study spoken to you personally?

    _____

    _____

    _____

    _____

    _____

    _____

Answers

1. a) 2   b) 3   c) 1

    d) 4   e) 6   f) 5

2. a) Instruction
    - The development of a disciplined mind.
    - Heightening our ability to concentrate.
    - Creating a growing awareness of our abilities and gifts.
    - Bringing a discipline to the use of our time.
    - Developing the basic disciplines of communication, i.e. reading, expression and research.
    - Growth in personal confidence as we progress.
    - Teaching us how to handle the things we dislike or find difficult.

    b) Experience
    - It provides a test-bed for our ideas, doctrine, and vision.
    - It knocks the rough edges off our character.
    - It develops practical wisdom in us.
    - It promotes self-awareness.

    c) Challenge
    - It shows us where our real security lies.
    - It provides fresh stimulus and inspiration, and it calls for the setting of fresh goals.
    - It provides a breeding ground for faith.
    - It prevents boredom and staleness coming into our Christian lives.
    - It enlarges our heart by causing us to become more open people.

3. See the relevant scripture(s)
    - In the development of life and character.
    - In the area of achievement and application.
    - In relation to the exercise of a particular gifting.
    - In the question of commitment and perseverance.
    - In bearing the responsibility of leadership.

4. See the relevant scripture(s)

    Growing in perseverance in the midst of persecution.

5. • Exposes the bedrock of our experience.
    • Highlights the true values of life.
    • Brings pressure which demonstrates our character weaknesses and strengths.
    • Develops our ability to persevere in faith.
    • Builds into our lives sensitivity and empathy.

6. • Exposing our own inner attitudes.
    • Testing our reactions to a whole range of different situations and attitudes.
    • Bringing our own fears and insecurities to the surface, and highlighting the threats we feel within ourselves.
    • Developing our capacity for personal relationships.
    • Providing a context for the growth of a servant heart in relation to others.
    • Challenging the possessiveness and selfishness within our own nature.
    • Teaching us how to handle people.

7. Personal

SECTION 9
The Value of Problems and Pressures

Introduction

In the world you will have trouble

Problems will inevitably come our way as Christians. To expect to live a problem-free Christian life is, to say the least, naive, especially if we are Christian leaders. God tailor-makes problems for us to enable us to grow in maturity in Him. He designs problems according to where we are at with Him and according to what we need to enable us to move on in Him. He will never present us with a problem that we will not have the resources in Him to handle.

Life can be looked upon as a series of problems. We can either learn from these or not, overcome them or not; but what we end up becoming in ourselves will be the result of the effect these problems have on our lives. Without the challenge that problems bring us, there would be no need for our faith to increase. Problems stretch our faith, because they often take us beyond our known experience, enabling us to grow in God.

We should be able to live victoriously in the face of any problem or difficulty that comes our way, just as Jesus did. This does not mean we will not suffer or find ourselves stretched to our limits due to problems or difficulties, but it does mean that God will be in them with us and that He will help us to stay in His will by providing everything we need to do so. We should not fear problems, but welcome them as our friends and as tools that will enable us to grow in God.

Key Verses

Matthew 5:10–12

2 Corinthians 1:3–7

2 Corinthians 4:7–12

Philippians 4:10–13

Hebrews 12:1–3

James 1:2–5, 12

PART 9.1
Bible Words for Problems

To understand what the Bible says about problems is not a simple matter. Instead of using the word *problem*, the Bible uses words like *temptations*, *trials*, *tribulations*, *hardships* and *sufferings*. These words can be defined in the following way:

- **Temptations**: this is mainly translated from the Greek word *peirasmos* in both the AV and NIV, and may be defined as either *trials or proofs with a beneficial purpose* or conversely *trials designed to lead to wrong doing*.

- **Trials**: this is translated from a variety of Greek words in the AV and NIV, and may be defined as *testings* or *the putting to proof the quality of things*; *a burning, a refining* or *a trial by fire*; or *being tried by suffering or temptation*. These mainly test our endurance and patience.

- **Tribulations**: this is translated from the Greek word *thlipsis* in the AV and can be defined as *great oppression, pressure, afflictions, or miseries*.

- **Hardships**: this is mainly translated from the Greek word *kakopatheo* in the NIV, and may be defined as *suffering evil, hardness, affliction, or trouble*. These tend to be more severe sufferings or privations.

- **Suffering**: this is again translated from a variety of Greek words in both the AV and NIV, and may be defined as *undergoing, experiencing or being subject to pain, loss, grief, defeat, damage, or punishment*. It can also mean *to permit to do, put up with, endure, or tolerate*.

When we look at the Scriptures, we can see that the early church lived with these things as a normal part of their Christian life (Matthew 5:10–12; Acts 5:40–42; Romans 8:17, 18; 1 Corinthians 4:10–16; 2 Corinthians 1:3–11; 6:3–10; 7:4–7; 11:23–33; 12:1–10; Philippians 2:1–18; 4:11–13; 1 Timothy 6:6–21; 2 Timothy 1:8–12; 2:3; Hebrews 10:32–39). In fact, the Scriptures suggest that Christian maturity is attained by living through and overcoming such difficulties.

Personal Notes

PART 9.2
The Bible Never Advertises an Easy Christian Life

No Christian would grow into maturity in Christ, if God did all the work for them. If He took all our problems from us and dealt with them Himself, if He made all our decisions for us, if He spoon-fed us and protected us from every difficulty, we would never mature in Him.

The Bible clearly shows us that life on earth is not going to be easy for the Christian (Philippians 1:29). We need to lean on God and rely on Him; and we need to be open to and receive the counsel and empowering of the Holy Spirit, but we must never run away or give up. God has always got what it takes to enable us to overcome even the most difficult of our problems. If we look to Him in the midst of our trouble, He will be there and He will show us what to do.

> *'We can rejoice, too, when we run into problems and trials for we know that they are good for us – they help us learn to be patient. And patience develops strength of character in us and helps us trust God more each time we use it until finally our hope and faith are strong and steady.'*   (Romans 5:3, 4 Living Bible)

PART 9.3
As Christians, How Should We Define Problems?

The traditionally accepted definition of the word *problem* is the one used in the Oxford dictionary. It defines problems as *doubtful or difficult questions or things that are hard to understand.*

The Greek word for problem, *proballein* (*pro* meaning *forward* and *ballein* meaning *to throw*), gives us a more interesting definition. It literally means *a thing thrown or put forward.*

God wants us, as Christians, to see problems in the light of the Greek definition. He wants us to see them as positive things. They are doors to answers! They are things that get us moving forward instead of staying where we are. They may be difficult, and we may even have to suffer due to them, but having overcome or learned from them, we will have moved on in God. In fact, without problems, we would get nowhere in God.

PART 9.4
The Three Sources of Problems for the Christian

i) God

Christians often attribute problems to the enemy, when in reality the source of the problem is God. He is giving us an opportunity to grow in Him and be more like His Son, Jesus. God has chosen us for His glory and not for our comfort. We should trust God and put our confidence in Him, no matter what problems or difficulties we face (Romans 8:28–30).

ii) Body and soul

There is a battle going on within us, as Christians, between our old way of thinking and acting, and that which God has done and is continuing to do in our lives. To overcome in this area, we need to yield our bodies and minds into God's hands. This requires self-discipline, self-awareness and a will that has God on the throne (1 Corinthians 9:24–27; Romans 12:1, 2; Ephesians 4:22–24).

iii) **Opposition**

Some problems find their source in the work of the enemy. Here we need to resist and even get into battle against anything which is opposing us as we seek to carry out God's will. Satan and his demonic horde are the main targets in this battle and it is foolishness to believe that he is not interested in us (Job 1:6–12; Luke 22:31–34).

Satan will attempt to crush us with problems, but we must remember that God is in control and that He will not let us be over-burdened, if we continue to look to Him and submit ourselves to His will. As long as we are living as God wants us to, we have nothing to fear from the enemy (James 4:7; 1 Peter 5:8–10).

PART 9.5
Twelve Reasons Why Problems Are Positive Things

- They expose the depths of our maturity in God. They show us where we are at with God and where we need to improve.

- They show us the true values of life. When persecution and difficulty come, it is not long before we know what is really important and what is just window dressing.

- They create self-awareness (i.e. show us who we really are) and highlight our character strengths and weaknesses (like metal testing).

- They develop spiritual perseverance. If we want to overcome or solve a problem, we have to press on and not give up. Too many Christians give up before they overcome.

- They build our sensitivity to and empathy with other people and their needs, because we learn by experience what it is like to be in their shoes.

- They refine and polish our gifts and capabilities. The pressure of problems knocks off our rough edges and drives out the rubbish within our lives, when we handle problems in God's way and in God's power.

- They develop our confidence in God rather than ourselves. We learn to trust God who always proves faithful.

- They enlarge our capacity in God and enable our faith in Him to grow, because they stretch us and create the need for us and our faith to grow.

- They test our securities. They teach us that we need to rely on God and that we can depend on Him (and often on not much else!), who is the only unshakeable, permanently stable entity.

- They stimulate us and prevent complacency. Problems are like a red-hot poker behind us.

- They enable creativity and help us to think and develop new ideas. They often force us to challenge 'the way we have always done it' syndrome and to come up with new and more effective ways of doing things.

- They develop wisdom, because we learn what God would do in our situation – if we wait on Him, rather than immediately reacting to our problems.

PART 9.6
God Wants Us to Grow Up

God is our Father and we are His children. At the start of our Christian life, He tends to protect and spoon-feed us because He knows we need it. However, He does not want us to stay in this place of immaturity in Him (Hebrews 5:11–14). He wants us to grow up!

He, therefore, presents us with challenges and problems appropriate to where we are at with Him, and He gives us room to learn by experience. He allows us to make decisions and even mistakes. Of course, He does attempt to instruct, correct and discipline us on the way, to teach us the boundaries of safety, to keep us on the right path, and to stop us doing the wrong thing or something that may be damaging to us, but He does not shield us from problems.

> **Read Hebrews 12:11–13 before proceeding**

Remember, God will never overload us with problems. He knows us better than we know ourselves and He will only allow problems to come our way that we will be able to cope with. The bigger the problem He gives to us, the greater the confidence and trust He has in us. God wants mature Christians who not only know what He would have them do in any situation, but who actually do it!

If He shielded us from every problem and intervened before we encountered any difficulty, we would never grow into maturity in Him. He wants us to not only know His truth, but live in the good of it. We, therefore, need to know that the truth works experientially. God gives us this opportunity by presenting us with His Designer-made problems and then giving us room to learn by experience.

PART 9.7
Problems Help Us to Mature in Christ

God knows that one of the best ways that He can teach us is to let us get some 'hands on' experience. This is because one of the most effective ways to learn is to present a problem and then let those you want to train work out the answer to it. Some basic ground rules may need to be explained to the people involved, but once they have understood these, they should be left to work out the solution to the problem themselves.

God uses problem-setting as one of His main methods to move us on in Him. His ground rules are given in His Word and He has promised to provide anything else we may need (2 Peter 1:3). God does not want us just to learn His truths off by heart (i.e. by rote learning, which is the poorest instruction method); He wants us to allow His truths to become part of our lives, and for us, as His followers, to apply them and live in the good of them. He encourages us to do this by presenting us with problems designed specifically for us. These God-given problems will take into account our level of maturity in Him and what we can cope with, and they will always be solvable, if we tackle them in His way.

As Christians, we need to see problems as our friends and teachers or as hurdles to overcome in order to grow into maturity in God. They are God's way of stretching our capacity in Him and increasing the depth of our faith. They can be thought of as mountains we need to move by faith, because every time we overcome them, it expands our faith boundaries and enables us to grow in God.

See Mark 11:22, 23

Personal Notes

PART 9.8
Problems Help Us to Develop Spiritual Muscle

Athletes train and force their body to do more, so that it becomes a more effective instrument for them in their chosen sport. They do this by setting hard-to-reach targets and pushing themselves until they can achieve them. This builds them up and gives them an increased capacity to achieve. Sometimes this pursuit of excellence is painful, but the athletes know that there is no gain where there is no pain. It should be the same with us and problems. We should see them as hurdles to overcome, which may cause us some pain or hardship, but will result in our moving on in God as we overcome them.

Problems can be thought of as the muscle-building tools of our Christian life. They help us to live a life that is always growing and developing, and which is dependent on God. God, by presenting us with challenges that we can only tackle with His help, is encouraging us to only do His will, because to step out of His will will move us into a place where He cannot give us the help we need. He is also helping us to live a disciplined Christian life, because we need to stay right with Him all the time in order to continue to live a victorious, successful, fruitful life in Him, which should be the aim of every believer.

PART 9.9
Four Problem Solving Steps

There are four steps involved in responding to problems in God's way:

- *Recognise* that you are confronting a problem. We should never 'bury our head in the sand' by pretending that there is no problem before us, when in reality one is staring us in the face and begging to be dealt with.

- *Receive* the problem or reject it according to your discernment of the source of the problem and what God's will is in this particular situation.

- *Respond* to the problem positively and wisely, using the accompanying pressure to motivate you to see the resolution of the problem.

- *Release* the problem once you have appropriated the answer to it.

PART 9.10
Two Important Principles

i) We need to harness the pressure accompanying problems

The dictionary defines pressure as *one body exerting a continuous force upon or against another that is in contact with it*. It is also defined as *a constraining influence*; or *an affliction, oppression, coercion, persuasion, trouble or embarrassment*. Another definition could be *that which comes upon us as a result of confronting a problem*. Pressure, if looked at in this way, can be a positive thing, as long as it is handled correctly.

Every time we confront a problem, there will be a certain amount of pressure placed upon us. The amount of pressure will depend on the size and nature of the problem and our ability to handle it. We need to learn how to harness this pressure in order to motivate us to resolve the problem. Christians, and especially Christian leaders, need to be able to deal with pressure in increasing amounts in order to grow in maturity in Christ and to do the work which God has set for us to do.

ii) We must not react to problems

Too many Christians simply react to a problem or the pressure associated with it and so rush into action or into decision-making. People who can never say 'No' to requests made of them, tend to suffer from this. God would rather we wait (when possible) and come to Him, seeking His counsel before we try to tackle any problem. This gives Him the opportunity to show us the source of the problem and to reveal His will in the situation. Making room for God in this way is essential, if we want to learn and grow into maturity in Christ as a result of the problems He allows us to take on.

PART 9.11
When Problems Are Resolved

Once a problem has been resolved, it is important that we release it. Christians often try to do more than God wants them to do with a problem. They hold onto it and refuse to give it up and, therefore, they step outside of God's will into sin.

Many other Christians fail because they let down their spiritual defence once a problem is solved. After a job well done, they relax and take their eyes off the Lord. This leaves them very vulnerable to enemy attack. Satan is no gentleman. He will wait for the moments when we leave ourselves undefended before he moves in. He often waits for the most inconvenient moments to attack us, e.g. when we are tired or upset.

We need to be always self-controlled, alert, aware of satan's schemes and on our guard, because our enemy the devil prowls around like a roaring lion seeking to destroy those who are weak or who have dropped their guard (2 Corinthians 2:11; Ephesians 6:10–18; 1 Peter 5:8, 9). It is alright to relax and look back on our successes in God, but it is wrong to move the focus of our eyes from Jesus and onto them.

It is also important to remember to thank God and give Him all the glory for problems successfully resolved. To do this helps us to keep our eyes on the Lord and our lives in perspective. This also helps us to resist pride, because we realise that we are humble servants of God, who depend totally on Him.

PART 9.12
No Overload with God

'No temptation has come your way that is too hard for flesh and blood to bear. But God can be trusted not to allow you to suffer any temptation beyond your powers of endurance. He will see to it that every temptation has a way out, so that it will never be impossible for you to bear it.' (1 Corinthians 10:13, J.B. Phillips Translation)

God does not allow us to go through difficulties and to face testing just for the sake of it. He wants us to develop a strong spiritual 'back-bone' which will enable us to stand up under any onslaught of the enemy and overcome any problem that may come our way.

He has enough Christians who are blown here and there by every wind of doctrine and who are flattened by every minor difficulty. This is not God's intention for any of His people. He wants us to discover His will and to do it, no matter what comes against us. He has promised that we will not be tempted or given problems beyond what we can handle and He also promises that there is a way out or a solution to every difficulty.

'And we know that all that happens to us is working for our good if we love God and are fitting into his plans.'
(Romans 8:28 Living Bible)

God is Sovereign. He knows everything that is going on. He is all-powerful and He is present everywhere. Nothing escapes His attention and nothing is too difficult for Him; and this God has His hand on our lives as Christians. He will not let anything happen to us that will cause us to fail, if we love Him and live according to His will and purpose. If we step out of His will and do our own thing, we can get into trouble, but if we remain in Him, we need fear nothing, because in all things God is going to work for our good. This is why Jesus says:

'Come to me, all you who are weary and burdened, and I will give you rest. Take my yoke upon you and learn from me, for I am gentle and humble in heart, and you will find rest for your souls. For my yoke is easy and my burden is light.'
(Matthew 11:28–30)

Bible Study: *Conflict and Confrontation*

The Scriptures make it clear that it will not always be easy being a Christian. We will face difficulties of conflict and opposition from sources that will sometimes surprise us. We do, however have Jesus as our great Forerunner and Example and the same Holy Spirit is available to us as helped Him. Complete the following scripture (Hebrews 12:1–3) to find out just how great an example Jesus is to us in this regard:

'Therefore, since we are _____ by such a

great _____ ,

let us throw off everything that _____ and

_____ ,

and let us _____ the race

marked out for us. Let us fix _____

_____ of our faith,

who for _____ set before him _____

_____ , scorning its

shame, and _____ at the right hand of the

throne of God. Consider him _____

_____ from sinful men, so that

you _____ .'

1. The Early Church

The early Apostles taught their churches to expect conflict and opposition. They did not do this to discourage them but to prepare them and to develop their spiritual strength so that they would not be overwhelmed by the reality of such difficulties.

'We must go through many tribulations to enter the Kingdom of God.'   (Acts 14:22)

Make a note from the following scriptures of the opposition the early Christians faced:

Acts 4:3 _____

_____

Acts 5:18 _____

_____

Acts 5:27 _____

_____

Acts 6:12 _____

_____

Acts 7:58 _____

_____

Acts 8:1 _____

_____

Acts 9:24, 25 _____

_____

Acts 12:2 _____

_____

Acts 13:45–50 _____

_____

Acts 14:5–19 _____

_____

Acts 16:22–24 _____

_____

Acts 17:5–10 _____

_____

Acts 18:6 _____

_____

Acts 19:29 _____

_____

Acts 21:11 _____

_____

Acts 22:25 _____

_____

Acts 23:1 _____

_____

Acts 24:1 _____

_____

Acts 25:1–2 _____

_____

Acts 26:1 _____

_____

Acts 27:1 _____

_____

2. There are many different reasons why believers face conflict and opposition. Discover some of them from the following scriptures:

John 17:15, 16 _____

Acts 17:6 _____

1 Peter 2:20 _____

Acts 28:22 _____

Ephesians 6:16 _____

2 Timothy 2:9 _____

1 Peter 4:4 _____

3. Opposition and persecution are often used by God for a deeper and more positive purpose. The Holy Spirit can turn circumstances which are meant to hinder or endanger to a greater purpose. We can learn from the Scriptures how adverse circumstances are powerfully used by God to bring about His own purposes in our lives. Note the circumstances described in the following passages:

    Genesis 50:20 _____

    _____

    Acts 8:4 _____

    _____

    Acts 16:16–40 _____

    _____

    Acts 22:11 _____

    _____

4. Spiritual conflict teaches us important lessons and gives us the opportunity to place our trust in God. What particular lessons do the following scriptures teach us?

    Matthew 5:44 _____

    _____

    1 Corinthians 10:13 _____

    _____

    2 Corinthians 1:8, 9 _____

    _____

    Philippians 3:8–10 _____

    _____

    1 Peter 4:17 _____

    _____

Answers

1. *Acts 4:3* – apostles were arrested and imprisoned.

    Acts 5:18 – apostles were taken into custody.

    Acts 5:27 – apostles were interrogated by the religious authorities.

    Acts 6:12 – Stephen was forcefully brought before the Council.

    Acts 7:58 – Stephen was driven out of the city and stoned to death.

    Acts 8:1 – strong persecution broke out against the church.

    Acts 9:24, 25 – Jesus spoke to the newly saved Saul – *'I will show him how much he must suffer for my name.'*

    Acts 12:2 – James (John's brother) was executed by the sword.

    Acts 13:45–50 – Paul was reviled, contradicted and driven away from Antioch.

    Acts 14:5–19 – Paul fled Iconium and was stoned in Derbe.

    Acts 16:22–24 – Paul was whipped and thrown into jail in Philippi.

    Acts 17:5–10 – an uproar broke out in Thessalonica; Paul fled to Berea.

    Acts 18:6 – Paul encountered opposition in Corinth. He was reviled by the Jews and brought before the judgement seat (verse 12).

    Acts 19:29 – an uproar broke out in Ephesus. There was controversy over 'the Way'.

    Acts 21:11 – Paul was warned by the prophet, Agabus, of the persecution which would arise in Jerusalem. Rioting broke out in Jerusalem and Paul was imprisoned.

    Acts 22:25 – Romans wanted to take Paul hostage.

    Acts 23:1 – Paul stood before the Council as a prisoner and was then taken to prison in Caesarea.

    Acts 24:1 – Paul was brought before the governor, Festus.

Acts 25:1–2 – Paul was brought before King Agrippa.

Acts 26:1 – Paul was sent as a prisoner to Rome.

Acts 27:1 – Paul handed into the custody of the a centurion called Julius.

2. *John 17:15, 16* – not of this world.

   Acts 17:6 – caused trouble all over the world.

   1 Peter 2:20 – do good and suffer

   Acts 28:22 – people everywhere are talking against this sect.

   Ephesians 6:16 – the flaming arrows of the evil one.

   2 Timothy 2:9 – my gospel, for which I am suffering.

   1 Peter 4:4 – suffered for the name of Christ.

3. *Genesis 50:20* – Joseph and his brothers.

   Acts 8:4 – Scattering of the early church results in mission to Samaria.

   Acts 16:16–40 – Paul and Silas in prison. Philippian jailer saved.

   Acts 22:11 – Paul's arrest leads to Rome.

4. *Matthew 5:44* – Pray for those who persecute you.

   1 Corinthians 10:13 – God will make a way of escape.

   2 Corinthians 1:8, 9 – We should not trust in ourselves, but in God who raises the dead.

   Philippians 3:8–10 – That I may gain Christ.

   1 Peter 4:17 – It is time for judgement to begin in God's family.

SECTION 10
More Than Conquerors

Introduction

The devil's tricks

In this section we continue to explore the subject of the problems that often confront us. We will define some of the particularly common areas of difficulty and also explore the promise of the overcoming power of God. There are some simple principles we need to bear in mind before we go further.

- The enemy will tempt us to take on problems that are not of God. He wants us to wear ourselves out doing unproductive things or be diverted from doing God's will. Even the best intentioned things in the world are dead works unless they are initiated by God. We must be careful to do only God's will, because taking on things outside of it will mean that we will not know His provision and backing.

- It must be remembered that even though we may face a problem which has been devised by the enemy, it has been permitted by God. When confronted with a problem, we need to discern the source of it and what God wants us to do with it, i.e. we need to discern His will in the situation and either take the problem on board and resolve it, or reject it.

- We, therefore, need to learn how to discern the difference between God's will and the enemy's. God is in control, and He allows the enemy to tempt us, but never beyond what we can cope with. God will show us what to do in every situation if we look to Him (Ephesians 2:10; James 5:13).

- Taking on problems that God does not want us to take on, will cause us to come under stress and introduce unwanted anxiety into our lives. Here, we will not have the resources in God to deal with the pressure which accompanies the problem and this will result in great personal stress. We need to deal with this by getting right with God and asking Him to forgive us for doing what we felt was right (or something which another person pushed us to do), instead of doing His will. We need to let the peace of God rule in our heart by doing what we know we should be doing in God (Philippians 4:6, 7; Colossians 3:15).

- Satan will attempt to push us too far, too quickly, resulting in a demotivated, burnt out Christian. God has given us a brain to use and the ability to reason, and we need to use these things when we assess what we should be doing in God in response to a problem. We need to be realistic. We need to know our strengths and weaknesses, where our talents lie, and where we are at with God. Trying to take on problems that are way above our ability to handle is foolishness, unless God makes it clear that we should. It is all right to be stretched by problems, but it is not sensible to be overwhelmed by them.

Key Verses

Romans 8:31–37   James 4:7–10

1 Corinthians 9:24–27   1 John 5:4, 5

PART 10.1
No Good Running Away

Many Christians today stay in a place of immaturity in God, because they refuse to take on the problems or trials which He has designed for them, to enable their growth into maturity in Him. When confronted with a problem these people:

- **get angry with God** and demand that He remove the problem from them. These people tend to complain all the time.

- **put up with a problem, instead of trying to overcome it**. These people tend to be quite fatalistic and suffer anything, because they believe it is God's will for them. They tend to be 'door-mats' for other people, the enemy and circumstances.

- *get depressed*, throw a tantrum and cry out to God for Him to take the problem away. These people tend to moan all the time.

- *blame satan* and get into battle against him, instead of tackling a problem and overcoming it. These people tend to get confused, disappointed and then disillusioned, because their battling often does not work.

The truth is that often a problem is God's response to the prayer of His people. They ask God to change them or to take them on into greater maturity in Him, and yet when He answers with the problem that will enable this, they do not want it.

This is usually because they have a preconceived idea about how God works or they expect Him to just miraculously change them. God is a loving God, and He will often let a problem which He has designed for a person remain for a time, even if that person does respond to it negatively, because He can see that this is the best possible thing for them.

However, if they persist in asking God to remove the problem, or they react to it in such a wrong way that it is beginning to damage their Christian walk, God will remove it. He often then lets these people have their own way for a time, but eventually He will take them back to that same problem, or another just like it, hoping for the desired aim to be achieved this time.

The tragedy is that many Christians have failed to go on in God, because they refuse to face and resolve the problems which He has designed for them.

PART 10.2
Ten Common Areas of Problems

God presents us with many types of problems to enable us to grow into maturity in Him. Answer the following questions prayerfully. They will help you to discover where you are at in God in the various areas.

i) Money

- Are you a good steward of the finances God has put into your charge?

- Do you live by faith in the area of finances?

- Do you see God as the source of your money or do you look to the world for your provision?

- Do you have integrity in the area of your finances or your church's finances?

- Do you know that you are doing what God wants you to do with your money?

ii) Sex

- Do you treat members of the opposite sex in the way that God expects (1 Timothy 5:1, 2)?

- Do you show proper caution when with members of the opposite sex, especially when you are alone with them?

- Is what you feed into your mind through TV, radio, books, magazines, etc. helpful or harmful?

iii) Power

- Do you regard leadership as a right or a privilege?

- Do you see yourself as a boss or a servant?

- Do you see yourself as proud or humble?

iv) Fear, worry and anxiety

- Do you have any fears that plague your life and that you do not seem to be able to overcome?

- Do you know that to worry is to sin, because you are not trusting in God and putting your faith in Him (Matthew 6:25–34)?

- Did you realise that fear is probably the devil's most effective weapon against Christians?

- Do you so want to please other people that you cannot say, 'No', when they ask you to do something for them, even when you know it is not what God wants you to do at that time?

v) Disappointment, discouragement and disillusionment

- Do you find that you want to give up and run under the pressure of disappointment, discouragement or disillusionment?

- How is it that Christians, who know God Himself, who have been saved out of darkness and who have eternal life, can be subject to these sorts of things?

- These things are often encouraged by the enemy, so what do you do about them?

vi) Competition

- Do you compare yourself with other people, or do you just get on with what God has called you to do and look only to Him?

- Do you see the success of other people in the church as a threat to your own?

- Do you enjoy the success of other people as they work for the Lord?

- Do you trust God, His Word and His promises to you, or do you look at the physical circumstances and trust them more, especially if they do not seem to be in line with what God has said?

- Do you find that you cannot fully overcome your doubts?

viii) Relationships

- Do you enjoy gossip, slander or misunderstanding?

- Are you still harbouring anger in your heart against anyone?

- Are you humble and forgiving?

- How do you deal with strife and friction? With love, or by burying the opposition?

- Do you see family problems as challenges to overcome in order to aid both your own and your family's growth into maturity in God?

- Do you see relationship problems as difficult things that you need to endure, or do you see them (as Jesus did) as an opportunity to display the fruit of the Spirit and the general principles of the Kingdom of God?

ix) Habits

- Have they mastered you, or have you mastered them?

- Is there anything outside of God that you could not give up?

x) Circumstances

- Do you control them in the power of God, or do you let them control you and your life?

- Do you bother to ask God what He wants you to do in your circumstances?

- Do you feel that God is big enough to cope with even the most difficult of situations, using you as the channel of His will?

PART 10.3
Overcoming

As Christians we need to learn how to respond to difficulty and challenge in God's way. We need to know how to handle life and to make the things that happen to us productive to the glory of God. We need to overcome our own limitations and so grow into maturity in Christ; and we need to learn how to handle success, as well as failure, so that satan has no opportunity in our lives through pride. Pride turns faith into presumption and causes us to demand our rights; and pride of life and position tends to become the motivation for our work and service. Even our successes need to die at the foot of the cross of Jesus.

> *'We are more than conquerors through him who loved us.'* (Romans 8:37)

As God's people we need to know where we stand in ourselves. We need to recognise what affects us, in what areas; and we need to know the overcoming power of Christ and where we need to alter our reactions and responses from the negative to the positive to enable us to operate without fear or favour in the zone into which God has called us.

This is not positive confession, which is often simply an attempt to cover over or mask what is really there in our life, instead of dealing with it. You cannot confess yourself into victory. Many Christians do not want to come face to face with the facts, so they live in a super-spiritual unreality, which renders them largely ineffective for God.

Instead of overcoming, these people pretend that their problems are not there. This often results in severe self-condemnation when things do not work out and their life persists to be totally lacking in freedom and togetherness.

> *'If you do not stand firm in your faith, you will not stand at all.'* (Isaiah 7:9)

We need to stand firm no matter what confronts us, and so know God, His ways and His power, that nothing can get on top of us. We need to be the head and not the tail, and we need to show other people that it is possible to live a victorious Christian life, not in our strength, but in God's.

PART 10.4
The World, the Flesh and the Devil

The main Greek word translated as *overcome* is **nikao** which means *to win a victory* or *to conquer*. As Christians, we need to overcome:

- *The world* – Believers have three options. They can struggle futilely with the world on their own; they can surrender to it and be enslaved by it; or they can obey God, entrust their life to Jesus, and live in the victory He won for us at Calvary. If we do the latter, there is nothing, apart from ourselves, that can stop us from doing God's will and overcoming the world (Matthew 16:18; Luke 10:19; John 16:33; 1 John 5:4, 5; Revelation 15:2).

- *Ourselves* – and our own limitations, and be those people God needs us to be. We have a tremendous inheritance in Christ and we should live in the good of it (Revelation 21:7). God will help us overcome, if we put our faith in Him and we look to Him.

> 'But thanks be to God! He gives us the victory through our Lord Jesus Christ. Therefore, my dear brothers, stand firm. Let nothing move you. Always give yourself fully to the work of the Lord, because you know that your labour in the Lord is not in vain.' (1 Corinthians 15:57, 58)

- *The enemy* – He who is in us is greater than he who is in the world (1 John 4:1–6; Mark 9:20–27). We are in Christ (Colossians 3:3), and He has triumphed over all the powers of the enemy (Colossians 2:15; Ephesians 1:17–23; Hebrews 2:14; 1 John 3:8). We can resist satan and he will flee from us, if our lives are first submitted to God (James 4:7). We need to stand firm in our faith (1 Peter 5:8, 9), and we need to overcome evil with good (Romans 12:21).

PART 10.5
Do Not Get Disqualified

The Bible often speaks of the Christian life in terms of a race (1 Corinthians 9:24–27; 2 Timothy 4:7). The Greek word for *race* is **agon** which means *conflict* or *contest*. It usually speaks of a contest or meeting of athletes, but it can also speak of an inner conflict of the soul, often as a result of an accompanying outer conflict.

The Christian life, like a contest or conflict, is not meant to be easy. Christians should never have a 'come what may' attitude to life, but rather they should be looking at life as having a definite purpose in God, and they should be living highly disciplined lives in order to achieve that purpose, just like any successful athlete would. God is training, moulding, maturing and disciplining us in order for us to fulfil the purpose He has for us, not in our own strength, but in His. In fact, He is training us to rely on Him, just like Jesus relied on His Father.

> *'Do you not know that in a race all the runners run, but only one gets the prize? Run in such a way as to get the prize. Everyone who competes in the games goes into strict training. They do it to get a crown that will not last; but we do it to get a crown that will last for ever. Therefore, I do not run like a man running aimlessly; I do not fight like a man beating the air. No, I beat my body and make it my slave so that after I have preached to others, I myself will not be disqualified for the prize.'*
>
> (1 Corinthians 9:24–27)

The Greek word translated *disqualified* in this passage is **adokimos** and it means **to be forced out of the race**; *rejected or castaway*; or *not standing the test*. Satan cannot get God to change His mind about us (Romans 8:38, 39), so he tries to divert us from God's purpose for us by tempting us to sin or do something contrary to God's will for our lives.

When satan has a foot-hold of sin in our lives, he will use it to lever us away from God's plan for our lives. We must not let him deflect us from God's purpose and so disqualify ourselves from the race. God may have invested a great deal of time and effort in us preparing us for a specific task, but He will not let us get involved if we disqualify ourselves. We may have been the best person for the job, but we will have to sit on the bench and watch someone else do it, if we break God's rules.

We need to keep short accounts with God and make sure that there is no sin taking root in our lives. To sit and watch as the moment God wanted to use us comes and goes, must be a very painful experience. We may try and do it anyway, as the children of Israel did after realising how wrong they were not to go up and take possession of the promised land (Numbers 14:1–45), but like them we will not get far and it will not really be worth our while (1 Corinthians 3:10–15).

> *'You were running a good race. Who cut in on you and kept you from obeying the truth? That kind of persuasion does not come from the one who calls you.'*
> (Galatians 5:7–8)

Jesus showed us the way to live victoriously in a world opposed to the Kingdom of God, and how to cope with the inevitable hardships and suffering. We can do the same if we follow His example and live in obedience to God (Hebrews 12:3). Jesus always seemed to know God's solution to every problem that was set before Him. This may not have been a solution that was easy to handle, but by taking this course of action, Jesus always stayed in God's will and therefore always in a place of victory. We are in Christ and we have the mind of Christ, so we can do the same (Luke 9:23; Colossians 3:1–3; 1 John 2:6).

PART 10.6
The Unshakeable Remainder

'At that time his voice shook the earth, but now he has promised, "Once more I will shake not only the earth but also the heavens." The words "once more" indicate the removing of what can be shaken, that is, created things, so that what cannot be shaken may remain. Therefore, since we are receiving a kingdom that cannot be shaken, let us be thankful, and so worship God acceptably with reverence and awe, for our God is a consuming fire.'　　　　(Hebrews 12:26–29)

God at this moment in history is shaking His Church in order to be left only with that which cannot be shaken. God carries out this shaking process by presenting His Church, and individuals within it, with problems.

These problems are not designed to cause the individual to fall from grace, but rather they are designed to point out things that need to be changed in them and in the church structures that they build. God wants us to learn that everything apart from Him is shakeable, and for us to put our confidence and security only in Him.

God wants to be left with mature, fruitful, righteous, and effective servants who will not fall apart or let Him down when He needs them. He also wants to be left with church programmes and structures that will enable His will to be done and not hinder it.

Bible Study: *Dealing with Problems*

L ooking at Romans 8:31–39 list the kind of problems Paul highlights. Note especially verses 35, 38–39. Alongside, where applicable, write down examples of those problems from your own experience (present or past):

Kind of problems

	Problem	*Example*
1)	_____	_____
2)	_____	_____
3)	_____	_____
4)	_____	_____
5)	_____	_____
6)	_____	_____
7)	_____	_____
8)	_____	_____
9)	_____	_____
10)	_____	_____

Example of problems

In Matthew 6:25–34 Jesus teaches about the specific problem of *worry* – something that affects all of us in one way or another.

a) What kind of things do people worry about?

_____

_____

b) What reasons are given by Jesus for not worrying?

_____

_____

_____

c)   In what sense are we:

   •   similar to those around us?

     _____

     _____

   •   different from those around us?

     _____

     _____

d)   What is the antidote to worry (verse 33)? Write it out in your own words.

_____

_____

Response to problems

How should we respond to problems according to the following verses?

   •   James 4:7:

     '_____ *yourselves, then to God.* _____

     the devil and he will flee from you.'

   •   James 5:13:

     'Is any of you in trouble? He should _____ *.'*

   •   1 John 5:4b–5:

     'This is the victory that overcomes the world, even

     our _____ *. Who is it that overcomes the world?*

     Only he who _____ *that Jesus is the Son of God.'*

In your own words, write a single phrase to complete this sentence:

We should respond to problems by

_____

_____

Word study: *overcome*

Look up the following verses. What does each verse say about overcoming our problems?

1)   Matthew 16:18 _____

_____

2)   Mark 9:24 _____

_____

3)   Luke 10:19 _____

_____

4)   John 16:33 _____

_____

5)   Romans 12:21 _____

_____

6)   1 John 2:13–14 _____

_____

7)   1 John 4:4 _____

_____

8)   1 John 5:4 _____

_____

9)   Revelation 17:14 _____

_____

Living with problems

Read 1 Corinthians 9:24–27 and then fill in the four blanks below:

'Do you not know that in a race all the runners _____ , but only one gets the prize? _____ in such a way as to get the prize ... Therefore I do not _____ like a man running aimlessly; I do not _____ like a man beating the air. No, I beat my body and make it my slave so that after I have preached to others, I myself will not be disqualified for the prize.'

a)   Why do you think Paul describes his ministry in terms of *running* and *fighting*?

_____

_____

_____

b)   Focusing on the image of the *race*:

- We prepare for the race by going into

  _____ (verse 25).

- What might this involve?

  _____

  _____

  _____

- We run the race being careful to avoid

  _____ (verse 26).

- How could this happen?

  _____

  _____

  _____

- We finish the race aiming to _____
  _____ prize (verse 25).
- The sad alternative is to _____
  _____ prize (verse 27).

Answers

Kinds of problems

1) Trouble
2) Hardship
3) Persecution
4) Famine
5) Nakedness
6) Danger
7) Sword
8) Death (e.g. bereavement)
9) Demons (e.g. oppression)
10) Future (e.g. job security)

Note: Don't worry if you have located more than 10 problem-areas from this passage!

Examples of problems

a) People worry about:
    – Life today: what we eat, drink and wear.
    – Life tomorrow: what the future ('tomorrow' – verse 34) will hold.

b) Reasons for not worrying:
    – We are commanded not to (verses 25, 31, 34).
    – God provides for us because we are valuable (verses 26, 30).
    – What does worry achieve anyway (verse 27)?
    – God knows our needs completely (verse 32).
    – There is a better way – seeking His Kingdom! (verse 33).
    – 'Today' is enough to cope with for now (verse 34).

c) • We are similar in our human needs for food and clothing and in the potential anxiety that can go along with such needs.
    • We are different in our priorities: in putting God's Kingdom before our legitimate human needs (and finding such needs met in the process!)

d) Antidote to worry:
    – Make sure first place in your life is given to living under God's holy rule!

Response to problems

See the relevant scripture(s)

We should respond to problems by humbly trusting God in prayer and by resisting the devil.

Word study: *overcome*

1) Being part of a church that will never be overcome.
2) Asking the Lord Jesus for the faith to overcome our doubts.
3) Exercising the comprehensive authority Jesus has given us over the enemy.
4) Receiving peace and encouragement from Jesus, despite worldly troubles.
5) Tackling evil by overcoming it with good, rather than letting evil dominate.
6) Growing strong in the spiritual battle by having God's Word within us.
7) Knowing that as God's children the incomparable power of His Spirit is in us.
8) Being born of God and continuing to exercise faith in His Son, Jesus.
9) Following in the 'wake' of Jesus' victory over the powers of evil.

Living with problems

See the relevant scripture(s)

a) Paul describes his ministry in terms of running and fighting because Christian ministry is rather like a competition with a prize on offer at the end. To win it requires disciplined training – in order that we 'get in shape' spiritually and stay that way.

b) See the relevant scripture(s)
   - Looking at the context this might involve a sense of:
     - Flexibility: being willing to pay for our own ministry and being able to adapt to where people are 'at' (1 Corinthians 9:12–18; 19–23).
     - Discipline: ensuring that we are not 'disqualified' (verse 27) by some of the temptations outlined from Israel's history. (1 Corinthians 10:6–10).
   - See the relevant scripture(s)

- By failing to 'hit' our God-given target (what God intends to achieve through us): in Paul's case reaching Gentile 'outsiders' with the gospel (Galatians 2:8–9).
- See the relevant scripture(s)
- See the relevant scripture(s)

SECTION 11
The Importance of Vision

Introduction

Our Great Need

> 'Vision is essential for survival. It is spawned by faith, sustained by hope, sparked by imagination and strengthened by enthusiasm. It is greater than sight, deeper than a dream, broader than an idea. Vision encompasses vast vistas outside the realm of the predictable, the safe, the expected. No wonder we perish without it!'
> (Charles Swindoll)

No significant life can be lived for God, nor can any significant work be done for God, unless it is grounded firmly on the reality of spiritual vision. God-given vision is what lifts Christians from the level of the ordinary and enables them to achieve great things for God.

Vision from God changed the direction of most of the Bible's major characters, e.g. Moses, Abraham, David, Isaiah, Jeremiah, Paul, etc. These Bible characters had an encounter with God which was more involved than personal revelation, they had a word from God that so took root in their lives that it issued in a lifetime of service and direction for God.

All people who are used mightily by God have a life-changing encounter with Him. It is almost as if God is getting these people's attention so that they will listen to Him and obey Him wholeheartedly for the rest of their lives. It could be said that the spiritual vision these people get from God takes hold of them and sets them up for life – all they can do is serve the vision God has given to them.

In this section and the next one we will explore two levels of spiritual vision. The first is *personal vision*, i.e. spiritual vision that God gives to us personally. The second is *corporate vision*, i.e. spiritual vision that may be sourced in an individual, but which affects more than just that person's life.

Of course, these two types of spiritual vision overlap. In fact, it is usually necessary to have a personal vision which fits into a corporate vision, because God rarely calls His servants to work for Him on their own.

Key Verses

Proverbs 29:18	Jeremiah 1:4–10
Amos 8:11, 12	Philippians 3:12–14

PART 11.1
Personal Vision

P ersonal vision is not the mystical experience many seem to have had through the ages of an apparition of Jesus or some similar thing. It is the movement of God's Spirit within a person's life which comes within a moment of human/divine encounter, e.g. at conversion or when we are called by God to ministry, etc.

Personal vision carries with it, not only the life-giving power of God's Spirit, but the seed of God's intention for that person's life from that moment onwards. Personal vision, therefore, carries with it its own imperative. There is something directive about it, even though the individual concerned may not see the details clearly for some time to come.

The idea of vision from God is something which many discount from their Christian experience. They are happy enough to have just become a Christian and, therefore, they have trivialised the work of God in their lives. They have reduced Christianity to the level of a small personal conversion experience, rather than the incursion of the living God of revelation into their hearts and minds.

Salvation contains the seed of the vision God has for our lives, i.e. God's vision for our lives is implicit in our experience of the saving power of Christ. He saves us from darkness by bringing us into the light of the Kingdom of His dear Son. He saves us from purposeless living by bringing us into the 'good works, which God prepared in advance for us to do' (Ephesians 2:10).

PART 11.2
Corporate Vision

All Christian mission organisations, churches, team ministries – in fact, every work of God should be founded on a corporate vision or revelation from God.

Corporate spiritual vision can be received by an individual, but it is not limited to that person alone. It is given by God to enable His will to be carried out by a group of people (remember, most of God's work is carried out by teams of people and not by individuals working on their own). Here, God releases His vision to one person and then catches other people up into it so that the vision can be fulfilled.

God may originally source a vision in one person, but generally He calls a team of people together to enable that person's vision to be fulfilled. This is not always the case, because some vision requires only one or a few people to fulfil it. However, when a large group of people are involved in fulfilling a vision, God will raise up a team of leaders to oversee His vision. God usually then only reveals the whole extent of His vision to this team of leaders.

Within any church or organisation, there are usually a variety of different works/visions going on for God at the same time, i.e. God has envisioned individuals to do certain works for Him. These individually envisioned people are also called by God to be part of the wider vision of the church or organisation, i.e. God has called them to outwork their vision within a wider church/organisation's vision. When this happens, the leaders of the wider vision rarely have the whole vision for their church/ organisation given to them as individuals. Instead, the team of leaders are constantly trying to piece together the jigsaw puzzle which when complete would reveal God's total vision for that group of people. While they are doing this, they need to keep things moving in the way God has already shown them is right for the overall vision.

PART 11.3
How Do We Receive God's Vision?

Personal Notes

God-given vision is the product of God working in us. He creates the vision and we simply receive it into ourselves. It then becomes a rallying point, or a goal which we move towards as His people. Vision is not a projection of what we perceive needs to be done or what we want to accomplish, but rather *it is a divinely sourced directive* which draws a response from us and calls us forth into action. Vision from God summons us!

Vision arises out of a burden to know and do the will of God and to become whatever God wants us to become. The questions are not, 'Where do I want to go?' or 'What do I want to do or become?', but 'Where does He want to take me?' and 'What does He want me to do or become?'

Vision from God can be seen, heard, experienced, personal, and prophetic. We need to spend time meeting with God and opening up our lives (and spiritual ears) to Him. Once we have heard from Him, we need to obey what He has told us to do (otherwise God's Word to us will tend to dry up). God will show every one of His servants the part He has for them to play in His time, if the person diligently seeks after Him. The truth is that this is the only way that we as Christians can live the fruitful, abundant, fulfilled lives that God promises us (Psalm 139:13–16; Jeremiah 1:4–10; Ephesians 1:4, 5; 2:10; John 10:10).

> 'Thou are the way, the truth and the life. Without the way, there is no going. Without the truth, there is no knowing. Without the life, there is no living.'
>
> (Thomas à Kempis)

Remember, God's vision for our lives will be revealed in His time, not ours. We simply need to get on with life, obeying Him and living in a way that pleases Him.

It was not until Moses was 80 years old that he received his corporate vision from God. Many years before this, Moses seems to have had an idea of what God wanted him to do, but this was a personal vision which had not yet reached its time in God to be put into action. God made Moses wait until His appointed time (He knew when Moses and the people would be ready). God's revelation has an appointed time for each one of us (Habakkuk 2:3).

Our job is to persevere until we are mature and complete, not lacking anything (James 1:4), and to be constantly open to God so that He can reveal His will to us.

> *'Consecrate yourselves, for tomorrow the Lord will do amazing things among you.'* (Joshua 3:5)

PART 11.4
Four Effects of God-given Vision

i) It is quickening (I am called)

It brings life, because it provides a life-changing thrust that brings new direction and purpose to our lives. Our life may have been heading one way, but once we have received God's vision, it grips us and we can do nothing but serve it. For example:

- Saul/Paul (Acts 9:1–31)

- Isaiah (Isaiah 6:1–8)

- Jacob/Israel (Genesis 32:22–32)

- Moses (Exodus 3, 4)

- Jerubaal/Gideon (Judges 6, 7)

- Abram/Abraham (Genesis 17:1–27)

ii) **It is motivating (I will/can)**

Vision from God makes us progress towards the goals that are implicit within it. If we have no vision from God, we will stagnate and perish!

In fact, vision carries the seed of God's purpose for our lives. The revelation Moses received at the burning bush contained more than merely a personal word for Moses, it carried within it the seed of God's purpose for His people.

Another example of a man motivated by God's vision was the Apostle Paul (Acts 26:12–23). It was not only the light on the road or the appearance of Jesus that changed Saul's life, it was also the directive that God gave him and that he obeyed. The experience opened Saul up to what God wanted to ask of him. It was when Saul saw Jesus that he was able to receive the directive, 'I have appointed you to go and to bring light to the Gentiles,' into his heart. In the experience of meeting with God, Saul received the direction for the rest of his life and it motivated everything he did from then on.

Later, the apostle Paul speaks of pressing on to take hold of that for which Christ Jesus had taken hold of him (1 Corinthians 9:24–27; Philippians 3:12–14). Paul did not have some cool little conversion experience which made little change within his life. Paul was aware of the radical life-changing dimensions of his salvation experience.

Remember, with God's vision goes the knowledge that we are able to fulfil our part of it, because God will provide us with everything we need (Philippians 4:13, 19; 2 Peter 1:3). We will also know that God would not have called us to go this way, if we did not have what it takes in Him to fulfil our part of His vision.

> 'Vision means that one sees a need in such a way that the possibilities of doing something about that need are far greater in one's heart than the need itself.'   (YWAM)

iii) It is constraining (I must only)

People who have truly received God's vision into their hearts from then on can only do things that are in line with that vision.

From then on their life is moulded and shaped by that vision. These people cut themselves off from their old life, and only want to do things which please God and enable the vision they have received from Him.

For example, the vision which Moses received from God was specific. It had outline and content, and he was not free to go beyond that outline or to alter the content. Moses was told by God, *'See that you make them according to the pattern shown you on the mountain'* (Exodus 25:40).

> 'When God gives a vision by His Spirit through His word of what He wants, and your mind and soul thrill to it, if you do not walk in the light of the vision, you will sink into servitude to a point of view which Our Lord never had ... You can never be the same after the unveiling of a truth. That moment marks you for going on as a more true disciple of Jesus Christ, or for going back as a deserter.' (Oswald Chambers)

iv) It is sanctifying (I will not)

People who get a vision from God get their act together. They begin to discipline their life in order to serve the God who has revealed so much of Himself to them. They no longer want to please themselves, but now want to set their lives apart for God and His service.

Moses was told by God, *'Put off your shoes from your feet, for the place on which you are standing is holy ground'* (Exodus 3:5 RSV). The thing that God did in Moses' experience was to cut him off, not only from his old life, but from any other plans or ideas he might have had. He could not live for anything else ever again.

PART 11.5
Vision Will be Tested

G od's servants will often find that their spiritual insight into the purposes of God and their vision from God are questioned, challenged or opposed.

They, therefore, need to make sure that they have heard from the Lord, so that they can see the situation with spiritual eyes of faith. In fact, God will often allow His vision and insight to be tested by allowing opposition to come, so that the believer can know just how deep their faith in what God has shown them really is. God wants His people to depend constantly on Him and His Holy Spirit, and not on their abilities/capacity/position, other people, or circumstances.

Another reason why God allows the vision He has placed in our heart to be tested is that He wants to receive all the glory for anything accomplished by the vision. God often tests us by causing the vision to hit a dead-end, i.e. after a vision is birthed, it will seem to die. There is nothing we can do in this sort of situation except go to God.

God allows such a situation, because He wants us to give the spiritual vision back to Him. After all, none of us should feel or believe that we own the vision we are imparting or working within. God wants all the glory; and we will find it far more easy to give God all the glory, if the vision of which He is a part, at some point, seems to die and is only resurrected by God.

PART 11.6
Loss of Vision

L oss of vision is not usually a problem for young, inexperienced Christians, because they see themselves in a place where everything is ahead of them. However, older, more established believers can find loss of vision a very serious problem, especially if they have completed their part of a spiritual vision. Here, the problem is that they have fulfilled one vision (or part of one) and failed to go to God to get (or be part of) another one. The main cause of this problem is that these folks have been doing a certain type of work for so long that it becomes part of them. Then, when this work is finished, they are at a loss, because their work was giving them meaning and a sense of purpose. Serving God, somewhere along the line had become secondary to doing their job. Such people, who once were busy, are now at a loss as to what to do. If this condition continues for too long, they often end up as lethargic, frustrated, cynical, disillusioned people. The answer, of course, is to wait upon God for fresh vision or for God to reveal in which vision He wants the person to serve Him.

SECTION 12
Finding Our Right Place

Introduction

Visionaries, enablers and sustainers

I n this section we will look at a very important aspect of the subject of vision, namely, the different types of people who are involved in it.

We will look, in particular, at the biblical example of Moses, a man with a vision if ever there was one! But even he was not alone. Moses was the source of creative vision (i.e. the *visionary*) for the people of Israel. He also had a number of *enablers*, e.g. Aaron (spokesman); Joshua (director, army captain, and Moses' aide since youth); Bezalel (craftsman, builder); Hur (uplifter); Caleb (encourager); and Jethro (advisor). The Exodus 3 experience did not belong to these men, only to Moses. These men were simply called by God to enable the vision that was sourced in Moses to become practical reality.

In Moses' case, his *sustainers* were the Levites, the sons of Aaron, the judges, the leaders of the 12 tribes, the master craftsmen/ designers, and the seventy elders, etc. These men were responsible for particular areas of activity in relation to the vision. The need for sustainers arose out of the areas of activity of the enablers.

All these three levels of ministry are necessary to enable God's vision to become reality. Of course, the areas overlap somewhat, but they give us an idea of how any God-sourced vision should be tackled and outworked. The secret is that each level of ministry has to take God's vision as it has been revealed by the visionary and make it their own. They have then got to get on and do the part God has called them to do to enable His vision to be fulfilled.

Few people are called by God to initiate vision (i.e. be visionaries) compared to the many who are called to serve the vision. The fact that there are fewer visionaries than enablers, and fewer enablers than sustainers is by no means a value judgement placed on the person or their ministry. The truth is that God calls all His people to do different things for Him and He is only asking them to fulfil that thing for Him. To try and do anything else is folly and usually will end up in failure and disaster.

God knows best, and we need to stick to what He has called and equipped us to do for Him. Remember, God's vision is the common property of all who participate in it (e.g. the Israelites in Moses' day), because this vision is God's and not man's. All the people called by God to work/participate within a vision have a share in it. It is not owned by the visionary.

Enablers and sustainers build part of a vision and, therefore, they need to see that they are indispensable parts of the whole that God will use for His glory. They should never see themselves as an individual doing their own thing in isolation. They should also never be 'Yes' men to the visionary, because they share with the visionary in the vision. Its success is their success! With the visionary, they all form a band of people who should move and flow in God's vision and fulfil the ministry/ activity that the vision creates for them as individuals to do.

Key Verses

Exodus 3:1–12   Exodus 31:1–11

Exodus 18:13–26   Exodus 35:34

PART 12.1
The Characteristics of Visionaries

There are a number of characteristics required by people who are called by God to source His vision here on earth. *Visionaries need to be people of*:

i)   Inspiration

Visionaries need to be inspired people and they need to inspire other people (inspired people tend to inspire other people anyway). If the visionary is not inspired by God, they will not be able to pay the cost of participating in and fulfilling their part of the vision, and neither will any other person.

Visionaries need to meet 'face to face' with God and gain His prophetic insight/vision and then transfer this to the rest of the people called by God to work within the vision. There is something magnetic about divine inspiration.

A visionary needs to be able to inspire other people to take on the vision and make it their own. When the visionary does this, he also needs to make room for the enablers and sustainers of that vision to be established and begin to function, i.e. they need to let God's vision operate/run freely through the lives of other people.

Visionaries need to be people of optimism and hope. J. Oswald Sanders reminds us in his book *Spiritual Leadership* that no pessimist ever made a great leader or inspired other people to take great action. The pessimist sees the difficulty in every opportunity, whereas the optimist sees the opportunity in every difficulty. In fact, it is usually the pessimists who hold back the visionary who is always wanting to push ahead. Of course, cautious/careful/prudent people do have a part to play in helping the visionary to be realistic, but they must never clip the wings of a person God has called to soar. Cautious people learn valuable lessons from history, but they are in danger of being chained to the past. The person who cannot see beyond their difficulties to discern the possibilities will never be able to inspire followers.

ii) Clarity

The visionary needs to be able to communicate the vision wisely and successfully, i.e. what the vision is, the strategy, details, etc.

To do this, they have to know and understand the vision. The vision has got to have definition to them, more than to any other person. Just as Moses received the pattern for certain parts of the vision God called him to work within (Exodus 26:30; 24:3, 4), so the visionary will need to spend time with God defining and bringing clarity to the vision God has given him.

The visionary can then tell the enablers and any other people who are called to be part of the vision what they are to do (i.e. what God's pattern is). Remember, people who have made the visionary's vision theirs, now want to be told details of that vision by the visionary.

iii) Understanding

Just like Moses, the visionary needs to understand the vision and its implications. They need consistently to know in their heart what the reality of the vision is and be able to judge/discern every situation that confronts them accordingly.

They, therefore, need to be able to see any kind of action/attitude/deflection that is deviating from what God wants for His vision and be able to bring people (and the vision) back to where they/it should be.

In fact, the visionary should be able to keep the enablers and sustainers in tune with the vision, and also understand and bring any adjustment that is necessary for the vision to be carried out effectively. Moses inspected the Tabernacle, because he understood what the vision needed to look like (Exodus 39:32–43). He made sure that everything that was done was according to God's vision given to him, because otherwise the glory of God would not come.

Visionaries need to be careful to remain as people of faith, and never to become idle dreamers who consider the affairs of the present beneath them or too mundane to bother with (i.e. become so high-minded that they become of no earthly use).

Visionaries also need to be people of foresight, i.e. have the capacity in God to see what lies ahead and make provision for it. They must be able to envision the end result of the activities in which they are engaged, and know what effect their policies, methods and goals will have on the future.

Personal Notes

iv) Authority

The authority of visionaries comes because of the anointing they have from God. They do not have to strive for this, but rather simply stand up in it. Other people will recognise it (especially those who are called by God to work within the same vision). If visionaries lose their anointing, they will also lose their authority and the right to run/source the vision. This is why those with vision always have to keep humble before the Lord.

v) Responsibility

Visionaries are ultimately responsible for the fulfilment of a God-given vision (no matter how many enablers and sustainers they have).

This means that they have to depend on the Lord and have faith sufficient to see the vision fulfilled. In fact, they need to be willing to take fresh steps of faith when there is seemingly only a void beneath them. Visionaries cannot pass the buck.

They need to count the cost of responsibility and pay it, in order to have the right to continue to lead the vision. It was Moses who had to continually put himself in a position between God and the people. Moses knew the tremendous responsibility of the vision and he knew the boundaries (and he nearly always worked within them). Visionaries also have a responsibility to point people to God and to His vision, and not to themselves.

PART 12.2
The Characteristics of Enablers

Just as God gave Moses able men to enable his vision, so God will give every true visionary every person they need to enable their vision.

The enablers take the vision one stage from the source and start to put it into action. They, therefore, need to be a very responsible bunch of people who can understand, organise, and clearly communicate the vision. They also need to be very close in essence to the heart of the vision. In fact, they should echo what the visionary is saying. ***Enablers need to be people of***:

i) Perception

Enablers need to be able to share in the vision and make it their own. They, therefore, need to be people to whom the visionary does not have to keep explaining the vision. In fact, enablers need to be people who can be trusted to interpret the vision to other people, to themselves and back to the visionary. They also need to see the issues involved in fulfilling the vision and be able to do something about them, i.e. make it work.

ii) Decisiveness

Enablers need to be people who are able to make decisions which are in line with the vision and which enable it to be fulfilled. Aaron had the means of making decisions for the Israelites over his heart (Exodus 28:30).

Enablers today need to know God and the vision in their heart and, therefore, be able to make the right decisions and enable the vision to be achieved (and never to deviate from it).

iii) Single-mindedness

Enablers need to be so committed to the vision that they keep to it (Joshua 24:15). In fact, they need to follow it until the end or goal is reached, whatever the cost to themselves. It was the two men who committed themselves to Moses' vision (and kept to it) that ended up carrying it on after Moses had died (i.e. Caleb and Joshua).

Enablers can be dangerous, because they are powerful people within a vision. For example, Aaron allowed dis-obedience and grumbling to deflect him from the vision when he created the golden calf (Exodus 32). Later, he

Personal Notes

deviated from Moses' vision by allowing grumbling against leadership (Numbers 12), and losing sight of the distinction between the holy/clean and the profane/unclean (Leviticus 10). Every time Aaron deviated from the vision, he caused much distress. The same is true for the enablers of most visions. They, therefore, need to be very careful to stay true to the vision.

iv) Motivation

Enablers need to be able to sow what they have got from the vision (at least in part) into the lives of other people, so that those people can and will get effectively into the action. They also need to have the ability to teach and motivate other people, so that those people can be useful to the vision (Exodus 35:30–35); and they need to be able to empathise with other people, so that they can enable them in the right way.

v) Leadership

They need to be leaders who can not only lead other people, but who also can lead and enable other leaders (Deuteronomy 34:9).

PART 12.3
The Characteristics of Sustainers

These are the grass-roots and the front-line people who put the vision into action and maintain it in practical and detailed ways. *Sustainers need to be people of*:

i) Submission

Sustainers need to be people who take the wider vision to heart, but who concentrate on working at their part of the vision. They, therefore, need to be in submission to the vision and to the leadership who are directing their effort to enable the vision to be fulfilled.

These people do not need to have a cringing, grovelling spirit which says, 'I am no good, I have no gifts/abilities and I must carry out every syllable that some divine prophet tells me!' They need to do the work just as the Lord commands them, and they need a true, godly sense of value and self-worth.

ii) Dedication

Sustainers need to be dedicated to finishing the task they have been called by God to do and they need to do this task to the best of their God-given ability. They also need to be people who will do the job even when they are left on their own.

iii) Willingness

Sustainers should have a willing heart to do the work that needs to be done (Exodus 35:20, 21), because they want to serve the Lord and the vision He has given to His people. They should also be willing to try and apply the vision to the context in which they are working.

iv) Perseverance

Sustainers should want to see their work completed well, and be willing to give of themselves and their time to enable this. They should also be willing to be stretched in faith and to pay the cost of this, so that they can carry out their part of the vision successfully (even if this means being stretched well beyond where they have been before). Jesus said, *'My food is to do the will of him who sent me and to finish his work'* (John 4:34). All who follow Jesus should follow His example in this area.

v) Gift

Sustainers will discover that they have the right gifts in God to do the particular task they have been assigned by God to do (Exodus 36:1).

In fact, a God-given vision will only be successfully fulfilled when each person God has called to work within that vision operates effectively in their God-given gifting. Visionaries and enablers need to be able to discern and release people into their God-given gifts/potential, so that the vision will be able to be fulfilled.

Remember, when people are released into their gifting, they are seen by others in a different light. All people who are part of a vision need to humble/submit themselves before the gifting God has given to other people within the vision.

PART 12.4
Areas of Overlap

M any of these characteristics can be applied to all levels of participation in the vision.

For example, just as there should be submission from the sustainers, so the visionary also needs to submit both to God and to the vision; just as the enablers should have perception, so sustainers need to see their place within the vision and know the value of that place; just as the sustainers need to be dedicated, so the visionary needs to be dedicated (in fact, he needs to be more dedicated, because he is the one who in the end will have to bear the greatest cost).

In fact, all the characteristics are inter-related, but it is the measure to which they need to be manifested that makes the difference.

Visionaries, enablers and sustainers all need to be servants of the vision; they need to have unity of heart and purpose; they need to have confidence/contentedness in their own place within the vision; and they need to be continually open in spirit to each other and to the Lord.

Everyone called to be part of the vision should also feel that they are personally related to it and to the visionary; they should know that they are personally accountable for what they do and, therefore, know a sense of worth and responsibility because of their work; and they should be personally involved in the message the vision is seeking to communicate, because everybody working within a vision should speak with one voice.

PART 12.5
Where Do You Fit?

W e need to be able to see ourselves and our work as God sees them. When we do this, we will be able to believe according to God's size and ability instead of being limited by our own size and ability. After all, it is not what we can do for God that counts, it is what He can do through us!

We each need to see ourselves as a person who is growing and developing in Christ and who is filled with the power of God. We need to have faith in ourselves in God (2 Corinthians 3:4–6; 4:7). It is only then that we will be able to achieve fully all that the Lord would have us do for Him. Remember, we need to have or be part of a big, God-given vision in order to achieve big things for God.

In the book of Exodus, we read of the craftsmen who worked with onyx stone. These men could probably do this job far better than Bezalel (although Bezalel probably knew the techniques). However, he as the enabler, got them with their gifting to be organised and he gave them a tremendous setting into which they could place their work.

The craftsmen and Bezalel needed each other to enable both of their jobs to be achieved. Can you imagine the day that they came to erect the Tabernacle? It would have been all in bits like a jigsaw on the ground. The onyx craftsmen and all the other workers would have stood there and watched as their piece went into the whole. Slowly the whole thing would have come together and the people I am sure, were amazed. Their little bit made up a part of the whole and was enabling a vision to be completed. They could have stayed as an individual doing their own thing, but alone they could not have even gone close to what they were seeing unfold before them.

Their work was a part of the whole in which the glory of God chose to dwell. We need to do our part for whatever vision God has called us to work within. That is the place where God's glory is going to dwell. In fact, it is a tremendous experience to begin to see your place in God's plans and how you fit into those plans in relation to other people of God.

God's people need to be content to do their part in the fulfilment of God's eternal plans. These plans, it must be remembered, go well beyond our lifetime. Much of what we envisage in God may not be work that we can achieve. This should not frustrate us or cause us to be disillusioned or cynical. We are only called by God to do our part in His plan and we need to be content in this. Even Moses never got to walk in the promised land.

Conclusion

Proverbs 29:18 could be paraphrased, 'Where there are no plans and goals based on God's word to a group of people, those people will drift into a meaningless, pointless, ineffective existence.'

If we are simply living for today with no thought for the future, then our life will just drift by with little achieved. We need to receive a vision from God which may be sourced in another person or it may be sourced in us. We then need to feed, nurture, and protect that vision, and anticipate its fulfilment by planning for it, i.e. we need to live out our lives seeking to fulfil that vision.

We should also expect the vision to unfold just as God has shown us it will. This is what faith is all about. Once we have or are part of a vision from God, we need to work at our part of it with all our might, along with the other people God has called to outwork the same vision. This means setting goals and aims and enthusing those who work with us so that God's vision can be fulfilled.

Some of us will be called by God to source a corporate vision, others will be called to organise and enable it, and still others will be called to staff it and keep it running. But all of us who have been called to be sons/children of God have a place in God's vision. If we want to be a success in God, then we need to be living in God's vision for our lives and we need to be playing our part within that vision.

Application of the Course

This section and the one before have dealt with the vital issue of *vision*. The following exercise will begin to help you articulate your own vision and see how you fit into a broader vision.

Perhaps you have heard the story of the man who came across three craftsmen working. He asked the first man what he was doing and got the reply, 'I am laying bricks!' He asked the next what he was doing and got the reply, 'I am building a wall!' Finally, he asked the third man what he was doing and he got an entirely different response. This man replied, 'I am building a cathedral!' The third man had caught the vision. He was doing his particular job, but he was doing it within the context of something far greater. Imagine his satisfaction when he saw the whole with his part in it!

How do you view your work and ministry for God currently? How **should** you view it?

_____

_____

_____

_____

_____

Do you need to seek God and allow Him to change your vision or to re-envision you?

○   Yes

○   No

Vision – levels

How clearly can you see your vision – for yourself **personally** and your team/church/organisation (**corporately**)? Mark your clarity of vision by circling the appropriate numbers below on a scale from 1–10; 1 being a 'very high' level of clarity and 10 being an 'extremely low' level of clarity.

	High									*Low*
Personal	①	②	③	④	⑤	⑥	⑦	⑧	⑨	⑩
Corporate	①	②	③	④	⑤	⑥	⑦	⑧	⑨	⑩

Past vision – reflecting

What is the biggest vision you have been a part of in the past years?

_____

_____

_____

To what extent has it been fulfilled? Is it in the process of being fulfilled?

_____

_____

Read the four effects (Section 11.4) again. To what extent was the vision you have just described:

		Very	*Reasonably*	*Not very*
1) Quickening?	(I am called)	☐	☐	☐
2) Motivating?	(I will/can)	☐	☐	☐
3) Constraining?	(I must only)	☐	☐	☐
4) Sanctifying?	(I will not)	☐	☐	☐

Present vision

What significant corporate vision are you involved in now?

_____

_____

_____

_____

Personal Notes

Articulate the vision of your church/team/organisation in a single sentence:

The vision of my church/team/organisation is

_____

_____

Are there significant differences between what you have written and the vision of the key leader/s? If so, what are they?

_____

_____

How would you describe your specific role in that vision?

_____

_____

Forward vision

'I press on to take hold of that for which Christ Jesus took hold of me.' (Philippians 3:12)

What is your personal 'that'? Is it clear or foggy?

_____

_____

In what way does your personal vision fit into a broader corporate vision?

_____

_____

Practically, are there ways you can prepare yourself now to play your part in this vision?

1) _____

2) _____

3) _____

Finding your place

Refresh your memory by glancing through the characteristics of visionaries, enablers and sustainers (Sections 12.1–12.3). Which of the three categories do you most naturally fit into? Mark the appropriate box below. You might like to ask other people who know you well if they agree or not.

Visionary   *Enabler*   *Sustainer*

❑   ❑   ❑

'A motor car has an accelerator, brake pedal and a gear stick. A team is the same. The accelerator is the visionary who is ready to reach ninety miles per hour in 6.2 seconds, leaving a cloud of dust behind him. On his own he would be dangerous – his pace and innovations would split the church. He needs the people who are brakes, to slow him down. Yet without the accelerator, the brakes would prevent real progress. The gear-changers are the wise men and women who can discern just when the church or group should move into higher gear, or drop down again because the venture has proved too risky.'

(Derek Copley)

Do you think this is true? What lessons can we learn from it? Is this any further help in determining your place in the vision you are involved in?

_____

_____

_____

_____

_____

Depending on whether you identified yourself as i) a visionary ii) an enabler or iii) a sustainer, answer the following questions:

1. Visionary

Place the five characteristics (Section 12.1) in descending order: the area you feel you are strongest in at number 1; the area you sense you are weakest in at number 5.

1) _____

2) _____

3) _____

4) _____

5) _____

Practically, how can you develop and grow in the area listed at number 5? Be as down-to-earth as you can.

_____

_____

_____

_____

Which people are your key enablers?

a) _____   c) _____   e) _____

b) _____   d) _____   f) _____

2. Enabler

As clearly as possible jot down the vision you are helping to enable in two sentences:

_____

_____

_____

_____

In what sense are you

- a strong enabler of the vision?

  _____

  _____

- a weak enabler of the vision?

  _____

  _____

What boundaries are you working within? i.e. What are the **limits** to your responsibility?

_____

_____

How would you assess your current motivation levels? (Circle the most appropriate number)

Very high   *Average*   *Very low*

① ② ③ ④ ⑤ ⑥ ⑦ ⑧ ⑨ ⑩

3. Sustainer

Assess your contribution to the vision you are currently involved in – according to the characteristics in Section 12.3. Jot down a number between 1 and 10 (e.g. submission 1 = 'very low level' and 10 = 'very high level').

Submission ☐

Dedication ☐

Willingness ☐

Perseverance ☐

Gift ☐

Fill in the following:

I believe my particular gifting is

_____

_____

My attitude towards my current task could be described as:

_____

_____

Proclaimers International is an international Christian ministry led by Dr Bob Gordon and based at Drayton Hall, Norwich, UK.

Dr Gordon is a prophetic teacher, preacher and author who has written a number of books on key issues in spiritual life.

The aim of Proclaimers International is to serve the wider Body of Christ and has three major emphases; Leadership, Discipleship and Evangelism in the power of the Holy Spirit. These elements of the ministry are expressed in the various strands of the work.

- **Proclaimers Spirit and Word School.** Full-time and part-time training courses are held continuously at Drayton Hall and welcome students from all over the world. The full-time course lasts for one year and consists of three terms. Students may attend all or part of the course which runs on a modular basis. The part-time course lasts for two years and is held one day a week. The School also offers distance learning courses which are available as printed material, computer diskette, audio tape or email.

- **Proclaimers Network.** An important networking of leadership, mainly in the UK, but some overseas. This Network is aimed at stimulating and encouraging leadership and providing a forum for discussion and spiritual insight on issues of contemporary significance.

  Proclaimers Network functions through a series of Forums held occasionally through the year at Drayton Hall and by means of a quarterly house journal, *Proclaimers*, which provides a practical link between leaders and provides articles of interest and challenge.

- **Proclaimers Resources.** A wide range of books, videos and audio cassettes are offered by Dr Gordon and other authors and speakers which reflect the heart of the ministry. These are available by Mail Order. Please see the main advert for details.

- **Conference Programme.** Throughout the year a diary of Special Conferences is held at Drayton Hall usually led by Dr Bob Gordon or other well known speakers. Full details of this programme can be obtained direct from Proclaimers International.

- **The King's Coach.** A unique evangelistic ministry which operates in other countries as well as Britain. This ministry operates with specially built vehicles which present the Gospel through a vibrant and interesting exhibition and also provide an area for personal meeting and counselling. The King's Coach operates in Europe and New Zealand as well as the UK.

- **Proclaimers International Ministries.** Linked with bases in the Netherlands, Germany, Uganda and New Zealand, which reflect the teaching and evangelistic ministry of Proclaimers International.

Foundations of Christian Living

This book has been written to help a wide range of Christians, from new believers to leaders of all kinds. It provides a practical, systematic study-guide to the fundamental principles of discipleship which will stimulate growth towards maturity. This book has made a terrific impact in many nations and has been translated into several major languages.

Master Builders

A valuable resource written especially for leaders and designed to encourage maturity and effectiveness within Christian leadership. It offers a 30 part study-guide which presents a balanced view of leadership with a clear, practical and spiritual challenge to all who desire to grow in spiritual responsibility within the Body of Christ.

The Disciple's Handbook for the Spirit-filled Life

This handbook teaches us about following Jesus in every part of our lives. Nine major sections focus upon key areas of Christian faith and experience: Discipleship, The Cross, God's Word, Faith, Fruitfulness, Authority, Spiritual Warfare, Ministry and the Holy Spirit.

Personally Speaking

Prophetic preaching is on the agenda again. The Word and the Spirit are the two main agencies by which God performs His purposes on earth. This book explores some important principles with regard to the dynamic revelation of the Word and the operations of the Spirit in inspiring and empowering human beings to share words of divine power.

Getting to Grips with God – *A two video series*

1. *Catching the Vision*. The two sessions on this video could change your life! They deal with the subject of spiritual vision and its implications for our life and work. For every Christian, as God wants to show each of us how to serve Him more effectively and how this can transform the most seemingly mundane and trivial task.

2. *Going for Gold*. A natural successor to *Catching the Vision*. The book of Proverbs tells us to guard our hearts for much of what holds us back is within – we need to take control of our inner lives in the power of God. Freedom in the Spirit requires that we be good stewards of our life and time. Bob Gordon gives some practical help to all who want to make life and time more effective in God's service.

For further information please contact:

Help Desk, Proclaimers International
Drayton Hall, Drayton
Norwich NR8 6DP
England

or visit our web site:

http://www.proclaim.org.uk

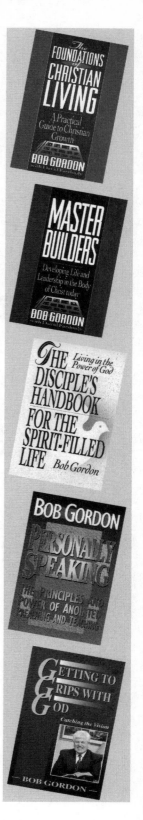